MznLnx

Missing Links Exam Preps

Exam Prep for

Linear Algebra

Fraleigh & Beauregard, 3rd Edition

The MznLnx Exam Prep is your link from the texbook and lecture to your exams.
The MznLnx Exam Preps are unauthorized and comprehensive reviews of your textbooks.

All material provided by MznLnx and Rico Publications (c) 2010
Textbook publishers and textbook authors do not particpate in or contribute to these reviews.

MznLnx

Rico
Publications

Exam Prep for Linear Algebra
3rd Edition
Fraleigh & Beauregard

Publisher: Raymond Houge
Assistant Editor: Michael Rouger
Text and Cover Designer: Lisa Buckner
Marketing Manager: Sara Swagger
Project Manager, Editorial Production: Jerry Emerson
Art Director: Vernon Lowerui

Product Manager: Dave Mason
Editorial Asitant: Rachel Guzmanji
Pedagogy: Debra Long
Cover Image: Jim Reed/Getty Images
Text and Cover Printer: City Printing, Inc.
Compositor: Media Mix, Inc.

(c) 2010 Rico Publications
ALL RIGHTS RESERVED. No part of this work covered by the copyright may be reproduced or used in any form or by an means--graphic, electronic, or mechanical, including photocopying, recording, taping, Web distribution, information storage, and retrieval systems, or in any other manner--without the written permission of the publisher.

For more information about our products, contact us at:
Dave.Mason@RicoPublications.com

For permission to use material from this text or product, submit a request online to:
Dave.Mason@RicoPublications.com

Printed in the United States
ISBN:

Contents

CHAPTER 1
VECTORS, MATRICES, AND LINEAR SYSTEMS — 1

CHAPTER 2
DIMENSION, RANK, AND LINEAR TRANSFORMATIONS — 27

CHAPTER 3
VECTOR SPACES — 38

CHAPTER 4
DETERMINANTS — 52

CHAPTER 5
EIGENVALUES AND EIGENVECTORS — 57

CHAPTER 6
ORTHOGONALITY — 67

CHAPTER 7
CHANGE OF BASIS — 73

CHAPTER 8
EIGENVALUES: FURTHER APPLICATIONS AND COMPUTATIONS — 78

CHAPTER 9
COMPLEX SCALARS — 91

CHAPTER 10
SOLVING LARGE LINEAR SYSTEMS — 107

ANSWER KEY — 116

TO THE STUDENT

COMPREHENSIVE

The *MznLnx* Exam Prep series is designed to help you pass your exams. Editors at MznLnx review your textbooks and then prepare these practice exams to help you master the textbook material. Unlike study guides, workbooks, and practice tests provided by the texbook publisher and textbook authors, *MznLnx* gives you **all** of the material in each chapter in exam form, not just samples, so you can be sure to nail your exam.

MECHANICAL

The MznLnx Exam Prep series creates exams that will help you learn the subject matter as well as test you on your understanding. Each question is designed to help you master the concept. Just working through the exams, you gain an understanding of the subject--its a simple mechanical process that produces success.

INTEGRATED STUDY GUIDE AND REVIEW

MznLnx is not just a set of exams designed to test you, its also a comprehensive review of the subject content. Each exam question is also a review of the concept, making sure that you will get the answer correct without having to go to other sources of material. You learn as you go! Its the easiest way to pass an exam.

HUMOR

Studying can be tedious and dry. MznLnx's instructional design includes moderate humor within the exam questions on occassion, to break the tedium and revitalize the brain

Chapter 1. VECTORS, MATRICES, AND LINEAR SYSTEMS

1. In modern mathematical language, distance and angle can be generalized easily to 4-dimensional, 5-dimensional, and even higher-dimensional spaces. An n-dimensional space with notions of distance and angle that obey the Euclidean relationships is called an n-dimensional _____
    a. Integer lattice
    b. ADE classification
    c. One-dimensional symmetry group
    d. Euclidean space

2. In mathematics, the _____ are the following sequence of numbers:

    The first two _____ are 0 and 1, and each remaining number is the sum of the previous two:

    Some sources omit the initial 0, instead beginning the sequence with two 1s.

    In mathematical terms, the sequence F_n of _____ is defined by the recurrence relation

    with seed values

    a. Fibonacci numbers
    b. -equivalence
    c. 2-bridge knot
    d. -module

3. In mathematics, the _____ of a ring R, often denoted char(R), is defined to be the smallest number of times one must add the ring's multiplicative identity element (1) to itself to get the additive identity element (0); the ring is said to have _____ zero if this repeated sum never reaches the additive identity. That is, char(R) is the smallest positive number n such that

Chapter 1. VECTORS, MATRICES, AND LINEAR SYSTEMS

$$\underbrace{1 + \cdots + 1}_{n \text{ summands}} = 0$$

if such a number n exists, and 0 otherwise. The _____ may also be taken to be the exponent of the ring's additive group, that is, the smallest positive n such that

$$\underbrace{a + \cdots + a}_{n \text{ summands}} = 0$$

for every element a of the ring (again, if n exists; otherwise zero.)

a. Coherent ring
b. Hereditary
c. Free ideal ring
d. Characteristic

4. In linear algebra, a _____ or column matrix is an m × 1 matrix, i.e. a matrix consisting of a single column of m elements.

$$\mathbf{x} = \begin{bmatrix} x_1 \\ x_2 \\ \vdots \\ x_m \end{bmatrix}$$

The transpose of a _____ is a row vector and vice versa.

The set of all column vectors forms a vector space which is the dual space to the set of all row vectors.

a. Normal basis
b. Symplectic vector space
c. K-frame
d. Column vector

5. In mathematics, in the field of group theory, a _____ of a finite group is a quasisimple subnormal subgroup. Any two distinct components commute. The product of all the components is the layer of the group.

a. Wreath product
b. Group homomorphism
c. Stallings' theorem about ends of groups
d. Component

6. In linear algebra, a _____ or row matrix is a 1 × n matrix, that is, a matrix consisting of a single row:

$$\mathbf{x} = \begin{bmatrix} x_1 & x_2 & \ldots & x_m \end{bmatrix}.$$

The transpose of a _____ is a column vector:

$$\begin{bmatrix} x_1 \\ x_2 \\ \vdots \\ x_m \end{bmatrix} = \begin{bmatrix} x_1 & x_2 & \ldots & x_m \end{bmatrix}^T.$$

The set of all row vectors forms a vector space which is the dual space to the set of all column vectors.

Row vectors are sometimes written using the following non-standard notation:

$$\mathbf{x} = \begin{bmatrix} x_1, x_2, \ldots, x_m \end{bmatrix}.$$

- Matrix multiplication involves the action of multiplying each _____ of one matrix by each column vector of another matrix.

- The dot product of two vectors a and b is equivalent to multiplying the _____ representation of a by the column vector representation of b:

$$\mathbf{a} \cdot \mathbf{b} = \begin{bmatrix} a_1 & a_2 & a_3 \end{bmatrix} \begin{bmatrix} b_1 \\ b_2 \\ b_3 \end{bmatrix}.$$

a. Dual number
b. Dual spaces
c. Polynomial basis
d. Row vector

Chapter 1. VECTORS, MATRICES, AND LINEAR SYSTEMS

7. The real component of a quaternion is also called its _____ part.

The term is also sometimes used informally to mean a vector, matrix, tensor, or other usually 'compound' value that is actually reduced to a single component. Thus, for example, the product of a 1×n matrix and an n×1 matrix, which is formally a 1×1 matrix, is often said to be a _____.

   a. Distributivity
   b. Self-adjoint
   c. Tensor product
   d. Scalar

8. In mathematics, for a given complex Hermitian matrix A and nonzero vector x, the _____ R(A,x) is defined as:

$$\frac{x^* A x}{x^* x}.$$

For real matrices and vectors, the condition of being Hermitian reduces to that of being symmetric, and the conjugate transpose x* to the usual transpose x'. Note that R(A,cx) = R(A,x) for any real scalar c. Recall that a Hermitian (or real symmetric) matrix has real eigenvalues.

   a. Vectorization
   b. Projection-valued measure
   c. Reality structure
   d. Rayleigh quotient

9. In mathematics, the _____ of two monic polynomials P and Q over a field k is defined as the product

$$\text{res}(P, Q) = \prod_{(x,y):\, P(x)=0,\, Q(y)=0} (x - y),$$

Chapter 1. VECTORS, MATRICES, AND LINEAR SYSTEMS

of the differences of their roots, where x and y take on values in the algebraic closure of k. For non-monic polynomials with leading coefficients p and q, respectively, the above product is multiplied by

$$p^{\deg Q} q^{\deg P}.$$

- The _____ is the determinant of the Sylvester matrix (and of the Bezout matrix.)

- When Q is separable, the above product can be rewritten to

$$\operatorname{res}(P, Q) = \prod_{P(x)=0} Q(x)$$

and this expression remains unchanged if Q is reduced modulo P. Note that, when non-monic, this includes the factor $q^{\deg P}$ but still needs the factor $p^{\deg Q}$.

- Let $P' = P \mod Q$. The above idea can be continued by swapping the roles of P' and Q. However, P' has a set of roots different from that of P. This can be resolved by writing $\prod_{Q(y)=0} P'(y)$ as a determinant again, where P' has leading zero coefficients. This determinant can now be simplified by iterative expansion with respect to the column, where only the leading coefficient q of Q appears.

$$\operatorname{res}(P, Q) = q^{\deg P - \deg P'} \cdot \operatorname{res}(P', Q)$$

Continuing this procedure ends up in a variant of the Euclidean algorithm. This procedure needs quadratic runtime.

a. Vandermonde polynomial
b. Touchard polynomial
c. Resultant
d. Padovan polynomials

10. _____ is the mathematical process of putting things together. The plus sign '+' means that numbers are added together. For example, in the picture on the right, there are 3 + 2 apples--meaning three apples and two other apples--which is the same as five apples, since 3 + 2 = 5.
a. ADE classification
b. Abelian P-root group
c. Addition
d. AKS primality test

Chapter 1. VECTORS, MATRICES, AND LINEAR SYSTEMS

11. In mathematics, _____ is one of the basic operations defining a vector space in linear algebra Note that _____ is different from scalar product which is an inner product between two vectors.

More specifically, if K is a field and V is a vector space over K, then _____ is a function from K × V to V. The result of applying this function to c in K and v in V is denoted cv.

   a. K-frame
   b. Scalar multiplication
   c. Symplectic vector space
   d. Matrix pencil

12. _____ is one of the four basic arithmetic operations; it is the inverse of addition, meaning that if we start with any number and add any number and then subtract the same number we added, we return to the number we started with. _____ is denoted by a minus sign in infix notation.

The traditional names for the parts of the formula

    c − b = a

are minuend (c) − subtrahend (b) = difference (a.)

   a. 2-bridge knot
   b. -module
   c. -equivalence
   d. Subtraction

13. In linear algebra, a _____ is a set of vectors that, in a linear combination, can represent every vector in a given vector space or free module, and such that no element of the set can be represented as a linear combination of the others. In other words, a _____ is a linearly independent spanning set.

   a. Supergroup
   b. Minor
   c. Chirality
   d. Basis

14. In mathematics, a _____ is a constant multiplicative factor of a certain object. For example, in the expression $9x^2$, the _____ of x^2 is 9.

The object can be such things as a variable, a vector, a function, etc.

Chapter 1. VECTORS, MATRICES, AND LINEAR SYSTEMS

a. Constant term
b. Tschirnhaus transformation
c. Coefficient
d. Vandermonde polynomial

15. In mathematics, _____ are a concept central to linear algebra and related fields of mathematics

Suppose that K is a field and V is a vector space over K. As usual, we call elements of V vectors and call elements of K scalars.

a. Groupoid
b. Left alternative
c. Hyperstructures
d. Linear combinations

16. In mathematics, the _____ of a number n is the number that, when added to n, yields zero. The _____ of F is denoted −F.

For example, the _____ of 7 is −7, because 7 + (−7) = 0, and the _____ of −0.3 is 0.3, because −0.3 + 0.3 = 0.

a. Artinian ideal
b. Additive inverse
c. Isomorphism class
d. Interior algebra

17. In mathematics, two vectors are _____ if they are perpendicular, i.e., they form a right angle. The word comes from the Greek ἀ½€ρθϊŒς , meaning 'straight', and γωνῖ α (gonia), meaning 'angle'. For example, a subway and the street above, although they do not physically intersect, are _____ if they cross at a right angle.
a. Expression
b. Embedding
c. Unital
d. Orthogonal

18. In mathematics, the _____ for a Euclidean space consists of one unit vector pointing in the direction of each axis of the Cartesian coordinate system. For example, the _____ for the Euclidean plane are the vectors

$$\mathbf{e}_x = (1,0), \quad \mathbf{e}_y = (0,1),$$

and the _____ for three-dimensional space are the vectors

$$\mathbf{e}_x = (1,0,0), \quad \mathbf{e}_y = (0,1,0), \quad \mathbf{e}_z = (0,0,1).$$

Here the vector e_x points in the x direction, the vector e_y points in the y direction, and the vector e_z points in the z direction. There are several common notations for these vectors, including $\{e_x, e_y, e_z\}$, $\{e_1, e_2, e_3\}$, $\{i, j, k\}$, and $\{x, y, z\}$.

a. 2-bridge knot
b. -module
c. -equivalence
d. Standard basis

19. In geometry, a _____ is a straight curve. When geometry is used to model the real world, lines are used to represent straight objects with negligible width and height. Lines are an idealisation of such objects and have no width or height at all and are usually considered to be infinitely long.

a. -module
b. -equivalence
c. 2-bridge knot
d. Line

20. In mathematics, a _____ is a collection of linear equations involving the same set of variables. For example,

$$3x + 2y - z = 1$$
$$2x - 2y + 4z = -2$$
$$-x + \tfrac{1}{2}y - z = 0$$

is a system of three equations in the three variables x, y, z. A solution to a linear system is an assignment of numbers to the variables such that all the equations are simultaneously satisfied.

a. Simultaneous equations
b. -equivalence
c. System of linear equations
d. -module

Chapter 1. VECTORS, MATRICES, AND LINEAR SYSTEMS

21. In mathematics, a _____ is a rectangular array of numbers. This way, matrices can record data that depend on multiple parameters. In particular they are used to keep track of the coefficients of multiple linear equations. Matrices are closely connected to linear transformations, which are higher-dimensional analogs of linear functions, i.e., functions of the form f(x) = c Â· x, where c is a constant. This map corresponds to a _____ with one row and column, with entry c. In addition to a number of elementary, entrywise operations such as _____ addition a key notion is _____ multiplication, which displays a number of features not encountered in numbers; for example, products of matrices depend on the order of the factors, unlike products of real numbers, say, where c Â· d = d Â· c for any two numbers c and d.
    a. Polynomial expression
    b. Heap
    c. Commutativity
    d. Matrix

22. In linear algebra, the _____ of a matrix A is another matrix A^T (also written A′, A^{tr} or ^tA) created by any one of the following equivalent actions:

    - write the rows of A as the columns of A^T
    - write the columns of A as the rows of A^T
    - reflect A by its main diagonal (which starts from the top left) to obtain A^T

Formally, the _____ of an m × n matrix A with elements A_{ij} is the n × m matrix

$$A^T_{ij} = A_{ji} \text{ for } 1 \leq i \leq n, 1 \leq j \leq m.$$

The _____ of a scalar is the same scalar.

- $\begin{bmatrix} 1 & 2 \end{bmatrix}^T = \begin{bmatrix} 1 \\ 2 \end{bmatrix}.$

- $\begin{bmatrix} 1 & 2 \\ 3 & 4 \end{bmatrix}^T = \begin{bmatrix} 1 & 3 \\ 2 & 4 \end{bmatrix}.$

- $\begin{bmatrix} 1 & 2 \\ 3 & 4 \\ 5 & 6 \end{bmatrix}^T = \begin{bmatrix} 1 & 3 & 5 \\ 2 & 4 & 6 \end{bmatrix}.$

For matrices A, B and scalar c we have the following properties of _____:

1. $\left(\mathbf{A}^T\right)^T = \mathbf{A}$

Taking the _____ is an involution (self inverse.)

- $(\mathbf{A}+\mathbf{B})^T = \mathbf{A}^T + \mathbf{B}^T$

    The _____ respects addition.

- $(\mathbf{AB})^T = \mathbf{B}^T\mathbf{A}^T$

    Note that the order of the factors reverses. From this one can deduce that a square matrix A is invertible if and only if A^T is invertible, and in this case we have $(A^{-1})^T = (A^T)^{-1}$. It is relatively easy to extend this result to the general case of multiple matrices, where we find that $(ABC...XYZ)^T = Z^TY^TX^T...C^TB^TA^T$.

- $(c\mathbf{A})^T = c\mathbf{A}^T$

    The _____ of a scalar is the same scalar. Together with (2), this states that the _____ is a linear map from the space of m × n matrices to the space of all n × m matrices.

- $\det(\mathbf{A}^T) = \det(\mathbf{A})$

    The determinant of a square matrix is the same as that of its _____.

- The dot product of two column vectors a and b can be computed as

$$\mathbf{a} \cdot \mathbf{b} = \mathbf{a}^T\mathbf{b},$$

which is written as $a_i\, b^i$ in Einstein notation.
- If A has only real entries, then A^TA is a positive-semidefinite matrix.
- $(\mathbf{A}^T)^{-1} = (\mathbf{A}^{-1})^T$

    The _____ of an invertible matrix is also invertible, and its inverse is the _____ of the inverse of the original matrix.

- If A is a square matrix, then its eigenvalues are equal to the eigenvalues of its _____.

A square matrix whose _____ is equal to itself is called a symmetric matrix; that is, A is symmetric if

$$\mathbf{A}^T = \mathbf{A}.$$

A square matrix whose _____ is also its inverse is called an orthogonal matrix; that is, G is orthogonal if

$$GG^T = G^TG = I_n,$$ the identity matrix, i.e. $G^T = G^{-1}$.

A square matrix whose _____ is equal to its negative is called skew-symmetric matrix; that is, A is skew-symmetric if

$$A^T = -A.$$

The conjugate _____ of the complex matrix A, written as A^*, is obtained by taking the _____ of A and the complex conjugate of each entry:

$$A^* = (\overline{A})^T = \overline{(A^T)}.$$

If f: V→W is a linear map between vector spaces V and W with nondegenerate bilinear forms, we define the _____ of f to be the linear map $^tf: W \to V$, determined by

$$B_V(v, {}^tf(w)) = B_W(f(v), w) \quad \forall\, v \in V, w \in W.$$

Here, B_V and B_W are the bilinear forms on V and W respectively. The matrix of the _____ of a map is the transposed matrix only if the bases are orthonormal with respect to their bilinear forms.

Over a complex vector space, one often works with sesquilinear forms instead of bilinear (conjugate-linear in one argument.)

a. Transpose
b. Tridiagonal matrix
c. Levinson recursion
d. Drazin inverse

23. In linear algebra, the _____ or unit matrix of size n is the n-by-n square matrix with ones on the main diagonal and zeros elsewhere. It is denoted by I_n, or simply by I if the size is immaterial or can be trivially determined by the context. (In some fields, such as quantum mechanics, the _____ is denoted by a boldface one, 1; otherwise it is identical to I.)

a. Orthogonal
b. Associativity
c. Artinian ideal
d. Identity matrix

24. In mathematics, an _____ is a statement about the relative size or order of two objects, or about whether they are the same or not

- The notation a < b means that a is less than b.
- The notation a > b means that a is greater than b.
- The notation a ≠ b means that a is not equal to b, but does not say that one is bigger than the other or even that they can be compared in size.

In all these cases, a is not equal to b, hence, '_____'.

These relations are known as strict _____

- The notation a ≤ b means that a is less than or equal to b (or, equivalently, not greater than b);
- The notation a ≥ b means that a is greater than or equal to b (or, equivalently, not smaller than b);

An additional use of the notation is to show that one quantity is much greater than another, normally by several orders of magnitude.

- The notation a ≪ b means that a is much less than b.
- The notation a ≫ b means that a is much greater than b.

If the sense of the _____ is the same for all values of the variables for which its members are defined, then the _____ is called an 'absolute' or 'unconditional' _____. If the sense of an _____ holds only for certain values of the variables involved, but is reversed or destroyed for other values of the variables, it is called a conditional _____.

One can apply the same algebraic operations to inequalities as one would apply for solving equalities. For example, to find x for the _____ 10x > 20 one would divide 20 by 10 to obtain x > 2.

a. ADE classification
b. Inequality
c. AKS primality test
d. Abelian P-root group

25. In linear algebra, functional analysis and related areas of mathematics, a _____ is a function that assigns a strictly positive length or size to all vectors in a vector space, other than the zero vector. A seminorm (or pseudonorm), on the other hand, is allowed to assign zero length to some non-zero vectors.

A simple example is the 2-dimensional Euclidean space R^2 equipped with the Euclidean _____.

a. Quasinorm
b. -equivalence
c. -module
d. Norm

26. A _____ is one of the basic shapes of geometry: a polygon with three corners or vertices and three sides or edges which are line segments. A _____ with vertices A, B, and C is denoted ABC.

In Euclidean geometry any three non-collinear points determine a unique _____ and a unique plane (i.e. a two-dimensional Euclidean space.)

a. -module
b. 2-bridge knot
c. -equivalence
d. Triangle

27. In mathematics, the _____ states that for any triangle, the length of a given side must be less than the sum of the other two sides but greater than the difference between the two sides.

In Euclidean geometry and some other geometries this is a theorem. In the Euclidean case, in both the less than or equal to and greater than or equal to statements, equality occurs only if the triangle has a 180° angle and two 0° angles, as shown in the bottom example in the image to the right.

a. -module
b. 2-bridge knot
c. -equivalence
d. Triangle inequality

28. In linear algebra, a _____ is an explicit representation of a vector in an abstract vector space as an ordered list of numbers or, equivalently, as an element of the coordinate space F^n. Coordinate vectors allow calculations with abstract objects to be transformed into calculations with blocks of numbers (matrices and column vectors.)

Let V be a vector space of dimension n over a field F and let

$$B = \{b_1, b_2, \ldots, b_n\}$$

Chapter 1. VECTORS, MATRICES, AND LINEAR SYSTEMS

be an ordered basis for V. Then for every $v \in V$ there is a unique linear combination of the basis vectors that equals v:

$$v = \alpha_1 b_1 + \alpha_2 b_2 + \cdots + \alpha_n b_n$$

$$v_B = (\alpha_1, \alpha_2, \cdots, \alpha_n)$$

This is also called the representation of v with respect of B, or the B representation of v.

a. Cofactor
b. Direction vector
c. Homogeneous coordinates
d. Coordinate vector

29. In mathematics, a _____ is an idealisation of the concept of a matrix, with a focus on the algebraic properties of matrix multiplication. The topic is comparatively obscure within linear algebra, because it entirely ignores the numeric properties of matrices; it is mostly encountered in the context of abstract algebra, especially the theory of semigroups.

Despite the name, matrix units are not the same as unit matrices or unitary matrices.

a. Laplace expansion
b. Matrix unit
c. Lie product formula
d. Logarithm of a matrix

30. In mathematics, a _____ in a (unital) ring R is an invertible element of R, i.e. an element u such that there is a v in R with

uv = vu = 1_R, where 1_R is the multiplicative identity element.

That is, u is an invertible element of the multiplicative monoid of R. If $0 \neq 1$ in the ring, then 0 is not a _____.

Unfortunately, the term _____ is also used to refer to the identity element 1_R of the ring, in expressions like ring with a _____ or _____ ring, and also e.g. '_____' matrix.

a. Ore condition
b. Unit
c. Ore extension
d. Ascending chain condition on principal ideals

31. In mathematics, the Cauchy-_____ the Cauchy inequality is a useful inequality encountered in many different settings, such as linear algebra applied to vectors, in analysis applied to infinite series and integration of products, and in probability theory, applied to variances and covariances. The general formulation of the Heisenberg uncertainty principle is derived using the Cauchy-_____ in the Hilbert space of pure quantum states.

The inequality for sums was published by , while the corresponding inequality for integrals was first stated by and rediscovered by

a. -equivalence
b. Schwarz inequality
c. 2-bridge knot
d. -module

32. In linear algebra, a square matrix A is called diagonalizable if it is similar to a diagonal matrix, i.e., if there exists an invertible matrix P such that $P^{-1}AP$ is a diagonal matrix. If V is a finite-dimensional vector space, then a linear map $T : V \to V$ is called diagonalizable if there exists a basis of V with respect to which T is represented by a diagonal matrix. Diagonalization is the process of finding a corresponding diagonal matrix for a _____ or linear map.
a. Hamiltonian matrix
b. Cauchy matrix
c. Pascal matrix
d. Diagonalizable matrix

33. In mathematics, the _____ is an operation which takes two vectors over the real numbers R and returns a real-valued scalar quantity. It is the standard inner product of the orthonormal Euclidean space. It contrasts with the cross product which produces a vector result.
a. Complex structure
b. Coefficient matrix
c. Centrosymmetric matrix
d. Dot product

34. In geometry, a _____ is a quadrilateral with two sets of parallel sides. The opposite or facing sides of a _____ are of equal length, and the opposite angles of a _____ are of equal size. The three-dimensional counterpart of a _____ is a parallelepiped.

a. 2-bridge knot
b. -equivalence
c. -module
d. Parallelogram

35. In algebraic topology, a simplicial k-_____ is a formal linear combination of k-simplices.

Integration is defined on chains by taking the linear combination of integrals over the simplices in the _____ with coefficients typically integers. The set of all k-chains forms a group and the sequence of these groups is called a _____ complex.

a. Bockstein homomorphism
b. Chain
c. Combinatorial topology
d. Tesseract

36. In linear algebra, the _____ of a matrix A is the collection of cells $A_{i,j}$ where i is equal to j.

The _____ of a square matrix is the diagonal which runs from the top left corner to the bottom right corner. For example, the following matrix has 1s down its _____:

$$\begin{bmatrix} 1 & 0 & 0 \\ 0 & 1 & 0 \\ 0 & 0 & 1 \end{bmatrix}.$$

A square matrix like the above in which the entries outside the _____ are all zero is called a diagonal matrix.

a. Complex Hadamard matrix
b. Main diagonal
c. Polynomial matrix
d. Diagonalizable matrix

37. In mathematics, _____ is the operation of adding two matrices by adding the corresponding entries together. However, there is another operation which could also be considered as a kind of addition for matrices.

The usual _____ is defined for two matrices of the same dimensions.

a. Matrix addition
b. Cofactor
c. Projection-valued measure
d. Nonlinear eigenproblem

38. The a-_____ of a string, for a a letter, is the number of times that letter occurs in the string. More precisely, let A be a finite set (called the alphabet), $a \in A$ a letter of A, and $c \in A^*$ a string (where A* is the free monoid generated by the elements of A, equivalently the set of strings, including the empty string, whose letters are from A.) Then the a-_____ of c, denoted by $wt_a(c)$, is the number of times the generator a occurs in the unique expression for c as a product (concatenation) of letters in A.
a. Weight
b. Presentation of a monoid
c. Trace monoid
d. Biordered set

39. In mathematics, particularly linear algebra, a _____ is a matrix with all its entries being zero. Some examples of zero matrices are

$$0_{1,1} = \begin{bmatrix} 0 \end{bmatrix}, \quad 0_{2,2} = \begin{bmatrix} 0 & 0 \\ 0 & 0 \end{bmatrix}, \quad 0_{2,3} = \begin{bmatrix} 0 & 0 & 0 \\ 0 & 0 & 0 \end{bmatrix},$$

The set of m×n matrices with entries in a ring K forms a ring $K_{m,n}$. The _____ $0_{K_{m,n}}$ in $K_{m,n}$ is the matrix with all entries equal to 0_K, where 0_K is the additive identity in K.

a. Normal matrix
b. Regular Hadamard matrix
c. Zero matrix
d. Complex Hadamard matrix

40. The set of all symmetry operations considered, on all objects in a set X, can be modeled as a group action g : G × X → X, where the image of g in G and x in X is written as gÂ·x. If, for some g, gÂ·x = y then x and y are said to be symmetrical to each other. For each object x, operations g for which gÂ·x = x form a group, the _____ of the object, a subgroup of G. If the _____ of x is the trivial group then x is said to be asymmetric, otherwise symmetric.

a. Symmetry group
b. 2-bridge knot
c. -equivalence
d. -module

41. In linear algebra, a _____ is a square matrix, A, that is equal to its transpose

$$A = A^T.$$

The entries of a _____ are symmetric with respect to the main diagonal (top left to bottom right.) So if the entries are written as A = (a$_{ij}$), then

$$a_{ij} = a_{ji}$$

for all indices i and j. The following 3×3 matrix is symmetric:

$$\begin{bmatrix} 1 & 2 & 3 \\ 2 & 4 & -5 \\ 3 & -5 & 6 \end{bmatrix}.$$

A matrix is called skew-symmetric or antisymmetric if its transpose is the same as its negative.

a. Stieltjes matrix
b. Symmetric matrix
c. Zero matrix
d. Butson-type

42. In its simplest meaning in mathematics and logic, an _____ is an action or procedure which produces a new value from one or more input values. There are two common types of operations: unary and binary. Unary operations involve only one value, such as negation and trigonometric functions.
a. Abelian P-root group
b. ADE classification
c. AKS primality test
d. Operation

43. In linear algebra, a _____ is a square matrix with entries being the unit fractions

$$H_{ij} = \frac{1}{i+j-1}.$$

For example, this is the 5 × 5 _____:

$$H = \begin{bmatrix} 1 & \frac{1}{2} & \frac{1}{3} & \frac{1}{4} & \frac{1}{5} \\ \frac{1}{2} & \frac{1}{3} & \frac{1}{4} & \frac{1}{5} & \frac{1}{6} \\ \frac{1}{3} & \frac{1}{4} & \frac{1}{5} & \frac{1}{6} & \frac{1}{7} \\ \frac{1}{4} & \frac{1}{5} & \frac{1}{6} & \frac{1}{7} & \frac{1}{8} \\ \frac{1}{5} & \frac{1}{6} & \frac{1}{7} & \frac{1}{8} & \frac{1}{9} \end{bmatrix}.$$

The _____ can be regarded as derived from the integral

$$H_{ij} = \int_0^1 x^{i+j-2}\, dx,$$

that is, as a Gramian matrix for powers of x. It arises in the least squares approximation of arbitrary functions by polynomials.

The Hilbert matrices are canonical examples of ill-conditioned matrices, making them notoriously difficult to use in numerical computation.

a. Minimum degree algorithm
b. Triangular matrix
c. Diagonally dominant
d. Hilbert matrix

44. In linear algebra, the _____ of a matrix is obtained by changing a matrix in some way.

Given the matrices A and B, where:

$$A = \begin{bmatrix} 1 & 3 & 2 \\ 2 & 0 & 1 \\ 5 & 2 & 2 \end{bmatrix}, \quad B = \begin{bmatrix} 4 \\ 3 \\ 1 \end{bmatrix}$$

Then, the _____ is written as:

$$(A|B) = \begin{bmatrix} 1 & 3 & 2 & 4 \\ 2 & 0 & 1 & 3 \\ 5 & 2 & 2 & 1 \end{bmatrix}$$

This is useful when solving systems of linear equations or the _____ may also be used to find the inverse of a matrix by combining it with the identity matrix.

Let C be a square 2×2 matrix where $$C = \begin{bmatrix} 1 & 3 \\ -5 & 0 \end{bmatrix}$$

To find the inverse of C we create (C | I) where I is the 2×2 identity matrix.

a. Unitary matrix
b. Unistochastic matrix
c. Euclidean distance matrix
d. Augmented matrix

45. In linear algebra, the _____ refers to a matrix consisting of the coefficients of the variables in a set of linear equations.

In general, a system with m linear equations and n unknowns can be written as

$$a_{11}x_1 + a_{12}x_2 + ... + a_{1n}x_n = b_1$$
$$a_{21}x_1 + a_{22}x_2 + ... + a_{2n}x_n = b_2$$
$$\vdots$$
$$a_{m1}x_1 + a_{m2}x_2 + ... + a_{mn}x_n = b_m$$

where $x_1, x_2, ..., x_n$ are the unknowns and the numbers $a_{11}, a_{12}, ..., a_{mn}$ are the coefficients of the system. The _____ is the mxn matrix with the coefficient a_{ij} as the (i,j)-th entry:

$$\begin{bmatrix} a_{11} & a_{12} & \cdots & a_{1n} \\ a_{21} & a_{22} & \cdots & a_{2n} \\ \vdots & \vdots & \ddots & \vdots \\ a_{m1} & a_{m2} & \cdots & a_{mn} \end{bmatrix}$$

Chapter 1. VECTORS, MATRICES, AND LINEAR SYSTEMS   21

a. Centrosymmetric matrix
b. Segre classification
c. Linear inequality
d. Coefficient matrix

46. A matrix equation in the form $\mathbf{Lx} = \mathbf{b}$ or $\mathbf{Ux} = \mathbf{b}$ is very easy to solve by an iterative process called forward substitution for lower triangular matrices and analogously _____ for upper triangular matrices. The process is so called because for lower triangular matrices, one first computes x_1, then substitutes that forward into the next equation to solve for x_2, and repeats through to x_n. In an upper triangular matrix, one works backwards, first computing x_n, then substituting that back into the previous equation to solve for x_{n-1}, and repeating through x_1.

a. -equivalence
b. 2-bridge knot
c. Back substitution
d. -module

47. A _____ is a symbol that stands for a value that may vary; the term usually occurs in opposition to constant, which is a symbol for a non-varying value, i.e. completely fixed or fixed in the context of use. The concepts of constants and variables are fundamental to all modern mathematics, science, engineering, and computer programming.

Much of the basic theory for which we use variables today, such as school geometry and algebra, was developed thousands of years ago, but the use of symbolic formulae and variables is only several hundreds of years old.

a. Variable
b. -module
c. 2-bridge knot
d. -equivalence

48. In mathematics, _____ refers to the rewriting of an expression into a simpler form. For example, the process of rewriting a fraction into one with the smallest whole-number denominator possible (while keeping the numerator an integer) is called 'reducing a fraction'. Rewriting a radical (or 'root') expression with the smallest possible whole number under the radical symbol is called 'reducing a radical'.

a. -module
b. -equivalence
c. 2-bridge knot
d. Reduction

Chapter 1. VECTORS, MATRICES, AND LINEAR SYSTEMS

49. In mathematics, an _____ is a simple matrix which differs from the identity matrix in a minimal way. The elementary matrices generate the general linear group of invertible matrices, and left (respectively, right) multiplication by an _____ represent elementary row operations (respectively, elementary column operations.)

In algebraic K-theory, 'elementary matrices' refers only to the row-addition matrices.

 a. Orthonormal basis
 b. Orthogonalization
 c. Orientation
 d. Elementary matrix

50. Let S be a set with a binary operation * . If e is an identity element of (S, *) and a * b = e, then a is called a _____ of b and b is called a right inverse of a. If an element x is both a _____ and a right inverse of y, then x is called a two-sided inverse, or simply an inverse, of y.
 a. -module
 b. -equivalence
 c. 2-bridge knot
 d. Left inverse

51. Matrix inversion is the process of finding the matrix B that satisfies the prior equation for a given _____ A.
 a. Overdetermined
 b. Invertible matrix
 c. Independent equation
 d. Orientation

52. Generally, in mathematics, a _____ of an object is a standard way of presenting that object.

_____ can also mean a differential form that is defined in a natural (canonical) way; see below.

Suppose we have some set S of objects, with an equivalence relation.

 a. Monomial basis
 b. Canonical form
 c. Cylindrical algebraic decomposition
 d. Brahmagupta's identity

53. In mathematics, an element x of a ring R is called _____ if there exists some positive integer n such that $x^n = 0$.

Chapter 1. VECTORS, MATRICES, AND LINEAR SYSTEMS

The term was introduced by Benjamin Peirce in the context of elements of an algebra that vanish when raised to a power.

- This definition can be applied in particular to square matrices. The matrix

$$A = \begin{pmatrix} 0 & 1 & 0 \\ 0 & 0 & 1 \\ 0 & 0 & 0 \end{pmatrix}$$

is _____ because $A^3 = 0$. See _____ matrix for more.

a. Hochschild homology
b. Ring of integers
c. Nilpotent
d. Product ring

54. In linear algebra, a _____ is a square matrix N such that

$$N^k = 0$$

for some positive integer k. The smallest such k is sometimes called the degree of N.

More generally, a nilpotent transformation is a linear transformation L of a vector space such that $L^k = 0$ for some positive integer k.

a. Nilpotent matrix
b. Main diagonal
c. Pascal matrix
d. Shift matrix

55. In the mathematical discipline of linear algebra, a _____ is a special kind of square matrix where the entries either below or above the main diagonal are zero. Because matrix equations with triangular matrices are easier to solve they are very important in numerical analysis. The LU decomposition gives an algorithm to decompose any invertible matrix A into a normed lower triangle matrix L and an upper triangle matrix U.

a. Circulant matrix
b. Hilbert matrix
c. Diagonally dominant
d. Triangular matrix

Chapter 1. VECTORS, MATRICES, AND LINEAR SYSTEMS

56. _____ is called _____ matrix or right triangular matrix.

The standard operations on triangular matrices conveniently preserve the triangular form: the sum and product of two _____ matrices is again _____. The inverse of an _____ matrix is also _____, and of course we can multiply an _____ matrix by a constant and it will still be _____.

a. ADE classification
b. Upper triangular
c. AKS primality test
d. Abelian P-root group

57. _____ is called _____ or right triangular matrix.

The standard operations on triangular matrices conveniently preserve the triangular form: the sum and product of two upper triangular matrices is again upper triangular. The inverse of an _____ is also upper triangular, and of course we can multiply an _____ by a constant and it will still be upper triangular.

a. AKS primality test
b. ADE classification
c. Abelian P-root group
d. Upper triangular matrix

58. In mathematics, a system of linear equations is considered _____ if there are more equations than unknowns. The terminology can be described in terms of the concept of counting constants. Each unknown can be seen as an available degree of freedom.

a. Overdetermined
b. Orthogonalization
c. Elementary matrix
d. Euclidean subspace

59. For each _____ of a linear transformation, there is a corresponding scalar value called an eigenvalue for that vector, which determines the amount the _____ is scaled under the linear transformation. For example, an eigenvalue of +2 means that the _____ is doubled in length and points in the same direction. An eigenvalue of +1 means that the _____ is unchanged, while an eigenvalue of −1 means that the _____ is reversed in sense.

a. Abelian P-root group
b. Eigenvector
c. ADE classification
d. AKS primality test

Chapter 1. VECTORS, MATRICES, AND LINEAR SYSTEMS

60. In linear algebra, the _____ states that every square matrix over the real or complex field satisfies its own characteristic equation.

More precisely; if A is the given n×n matrix and I_n is the n×n identity matrix, then the characteristic polynomial of A is defined as:

where 'det' is the determinant function. The _____ states that substituting the matrix A in the characteristic polynomial (which involves multiplying its constant term by I_n, since that is the zeroth power of A) results in the zero matrix:

The _____ also holds for square matrices over commutative rings.

a. Cayley-Hamilton theorem
b. -module
c. -equivalence
d. 2-bridge knot

61. In algebra, a commutative ring R is said to be _____ if any of the following equivalent conditions holds:

1. The localization $R_\mathfrak{m}$ of R at $\mathfrak{m}$ is a valuation ring for every maximal ideal $\mathfrak{m}$ of R.
2. For all ideals $\mathfrak{a}, \mathfrak{b}$, and $\mathfrak{c}$,

$$\mathfrak{a} \cap (\mathfrak{b} + \mathfrak{c}) = (\mathfrak{a} \cap \mathfrak{b}) + (\mathfrak{a} \cap \mathfrak{c})$$

- For all ideals $\mathfrak{a}, \mathfrak{b}$, and $\mathfrak{c}$,

$$\mathfrak{a} + (\mathfrak{b} \cap \mathfrak{c}) = (\mathfrak{a} + \mathfrak{b}) \cap (\mathfrak{a} + \mathfrak{c})$$

An _____ domain is called a Prüfer domain.

a. Exchange matrix
b. Arithmetical
c. Inverse eigenvalues theorem
d. Ordered vector space

Chapter 1. VECTORS, MATRICES, AND LINEAR SYSTEMS

62. In abstract algebra, the _____ of a module is a measure of the module's 'size'. It is defined as the _____ of the longest ascending chain of submodules and is a generalization of the concept of dimension for vector spaces. The modules with finite _____ share many important properties with finite-dimensional vector spaces.
    a. Supermodule
    b. Length
    c. Finitely generated module
    d. Morita equivalence

63. A _____ is a set G closed under a binary operation · satisfying the following 3 axioms:

    - Associativity: For all a, b and c in G, (a · b) · c = a · (b · c.)
    - Identity element: There exists an e∈G such that for all a in G, e · a = a · e = a.
    - Inverse element: For each a in G, there is an element b in G such that a · b = b · a = e, where e is an identity element.

    Basic examples for groups are the integers Z with addition operation, or rational numbers without zero Q{0} with multiplication. More generally, for any ring R, the units in R form a multiplicative _____ Groups include, however, much more general structures than the above.

    a. Product of group subsets
    b. Grigorchuk group
    c. Group
    d. Nilpotent group

Chapter 2. DIMENSION, RANK, AND LINEAR TRANSFORMATIONS

1. In linear algebra, a family of vectors is _____ if none of them can be written as a linear combination of finitely many other vectors in the collection. A family of vectors which is not _____ is called linearly dependent. For instance, in the three-dimensional real vector space $\mathbb{R}^3$ we have the following example.
   a. Derivative algebra
   b. Grothendieck group
   c. Linearly independent
   d. Composition ring

2. In mathematics, a _____ is a rectangular array of numbers. This way, matrices can record data that depend on multiple parameters. In particular they are used to keep track of the coefficients of multiple linear equations. Matrices are closely connected to linear transformations, which are higher-dimensional analogs of linear functions, i.e., functions of the form f(x) = c Â· x, where c is a constant. This map corresponds to a _____ with one row and column, with entry c. In addition to a number of elementary, entrywise operations such as _____ addition a key notion is _____ multiplication, which displays a number of features not encountered in numbers; for example, products of matrices depend on the order of the factors, unlike products of real numbers, say, where c Â· d = d Â· c for any two numbers c and d.
   a. Commutativity
   b. Matrix
   c. Polynomial expression
   d. Heap

3. In linear algebra, a square matrix A is called diagonalizable if it is similar to a diagonal matrix, i.e., if there exists an invertible matrix P such that $P^{-1}AP$ is a diagonal matrix. If V is a finite-dimensional vector space, then a linear map T : V → V is called diagonalizable if there exists a basis of V with respect to which T is represented by a diagonal matrix. Diagonalization is the process of finding a corresponding diagonal matrix for a _____ or linear map.
   a. Pascal matrix
   b. Cauchy matrix
   c. Hamiltonian matrix
   d. Diagonalizable matrix

4. In mathematics, the _____ of a vector space V is the cardinality (i.e. the number of vectors) of a basis of V. It is sometimes called Hamel _____ or algebraic _____ to distinguish it from other types of _____. All bases of a vector space have equal cardinality and so the _____ of a vector space is uniquely defined. The _____ of the vector space V over the field F can be written as $\dim_F(V)$ or as [V : F], read '_____ of V over F'.
   a. Cofactor
   b. Dimension
   c. Dual basis
   d. Partial trace

Chapter 2. DIMENSION, RANK, AND LINEAR TRANSFORMATIONS

5. The column _____ of a matrix A is the maximal number of linearly independent columns of A. Likewise, the row _____ is the maximal number of linearly independent rows of A.

Since the column _____ and the row _____ are always equal, they are simply called the _____ of A. More abstractly, it is the dimension of the image of A. For the proofs, see, e.g., Murase (1960), Andrea ' Wong (1960), Williams ' Cater (1968), Mackiw (1995).) It is commonly denoted by either rk(A) or _____ A.

a. Schur complement
b. Rank
c. Generalized Pauli matrices
d. Split-complex number

6. In mathematics, especially in the area of abstract algebra known as ring theory, a _____ is a ring with $0 \neq 1$ such that ab = 0 implies that either a = 0 or b = 0 (the zero-product property.) That is, it is a nontrivial ring without left or right zero divisors. A commutative _____ is called an integral _____.

a. Coherent ring
b. Partially-ordered ring
c. Subring
d. Domain

7. In linear algebra, the _____ or unit matrix of size n is the n-by-n square matrix with ones on the main diagonal and zeros elsewhere. It is denoted by I_n, or simply by I if the size is immaterial or can be trivially determined by the context. (In some fields, such as quantum mechanics, the _____ is denoted by a boldface one, 1; otherwise it is identical to I.)

a. Associativity
b. Orthogonal
c. Artinian ideal
d. Identity matrix

8. In linear algebra, a _____ or row matrix is a 1 × n matrix, that is, a matrix consisting of a single row:

$$\mathbf{x} = \begin{bmatrix} x_1 & x_2 & \ldots & x_m \end{bmatrix}.$$

The transpose of a _____ is a column vector:

$$\begin{bmatrix} x_1 \\ x_2 \\ \vdots \\ x_m \end{bmatrix} = \begin{bmatrix} x_1 & x_2 & \ldots & x_m \end{bmatrix}^T.$$

The set of all row vectors forms a vector space which is the dual space to the set of all column vectors.

Row vectors are sometimes written using the following non-standard notation:

$$\mathbf{x} = \begin{bmatrix} x_1, x_2, \ldots, x_m \end{bmatrix}.$$

- Matrix multiplication involves the action of multiplying each _____ of one matrix by each column vector of another matrix.

- The dot product of two vectors a and b is equivalent to multiplying the _____ representation of a by the column vector representation of b:

$$\mathbf{a} \cdot \mathbf{b} = \begin{bmatrix} a_1 & a_2 & a_3 \end{bmatrix} \begin{bmatrix} b_1 \\ b_2 \\ b_3 \end{bmatrix}.$$

a. Row vector
b. Polynomial basis
c. Dual spaces
d. Dual number

9. A _____ is a method used by a computer language to store matrices of more than one dimension in memory.

Fortran and C use different schemes. Fortran uses 'Column Major', in which all the elements for a given column are stored contiguously in memory.

a. Skew-Hermitian matrix
b. Moment matrix
c. Polynomial matrix
d. Matrix representation

10. In mathematics, a _____ is a function between two vector spaces that preserves the operations of vector addition and scalar multiplication. The expression 'linear operator' is in especially common use, for linear maps from a vector space to itself In advanced mathematics, the definition of linear function coincides with the definition of _____.

a. Rotation
b. Linear map
c. Homomorphic secret sharing
d. Real matrices

11. In the various branches of mathematics that fall under the heading of abstract algebra, the _____ of a homomorphism measures the degree to which the homomorphism fails to be injective. An important special case is the _____ of a matrix, also called the null space.

The definition of _____ takes various forms in various contexts.

a. Completing the square
b. Monomial basis
c. Kernel
d. K-theory

12. In linear algebra, a _____ or column matrix is an m × 1 matrix, i.e. a matrix consisting of a single column of m elements.

$$\mathbf{x} = \begin{bmatrix} x_1 \\ x_2 \\ \vdots \\ x_m \end{bmatrix}$$

The transpose of a _____ is a row vector and vice versa.

The set of all column vectors forms a vector space which is the dual space to the set of all row vectors.

a. Symplectic vector space
b. Normal basis
c. Column vector
d. K-frame

13. In mathematics, a _____ represents the application of one function to the results of another. For instance, the functions f: X → Y and g: Y → Z can be composed by first computing f(x) and then applying a function g to the output of f(x.)

Thus one obtains a function g ∘ f: X → Z defined by (g ∘ f)(x) = g(f(x)) for all x in X. The notation g ∘ f is read as 'g circle f', or 'g composed with f', 'g after f', 'g following f', or just 'g of f'.

a. Linear map
b. Reflection
c. Shear mappings
d. Composite function

14. Let S be a set with a binary operation * . If e is an identity element of (S, *) and a * b = e, then a is called a _____ of b and b is called a right inverse of a. If an element x is both a _____ and a right inverse of y, then x is called a two-sided inverse, or simply an inverse, of y.

a. -equivalence
b. Left inverse
c. 2-bridge knot
d. -module

15. In mathematics, two vectors are _____ if they are perpendicular, i.e., they form a right angle. The word comes from the Greek ἀρθός , meaning 'straight', and γωνία (gonia), meaning 'angle'. For example, a subway and the street above, although they do not physically intersect, are _____ if they cross at a right angle.

a. Orthogonal
b. Unital
c. Expression
d. Embedding

16. In mathematics, a _____ is a flat surface. Planes can arise as subspaces of some higher dimensional space, as with the walls of a room, or they may enjoy an independent existence in their own right, as in the setting of Euclidean geometry

a. Similarity
b. -equivalence
c. -module
d. Plane

17. In linear algebra and functional analysis, a _____ is a linear transformation P from a vector space to itself such that $P^2 = P$. It leaves its image unchanged. Though abstract, this definition of '_____' formalizes and generalizes the idea of graphical _____.
    a. C_0-semigroup
    b. Projection
    c. Lumer-Phillips theorem
    d. Convolution power

18. In geometry and linear algebra, a _____ is a transformation in a plane or in space that describes the motion of a rigid body around a fixed point. A _____ is different from a translation, which has no fixed points, and from a reflection, which 'flips' the bodies it is transforming. A _____ and the above-mentioned transformations are isometries; they leave the distance between any two points unchanged after the transformation.
    a. Real matrices
    b. Shear mappings
    c. Rotation
    d. Reflection

19. In mathematics, for a given complex Hermitian matrix A and nonzero vector x, the _____ R(A,x) is defined as:

$$\frac{x^* A x}{x^* x}.$$

For real matrices and vectors, the condition of being Hermitian reduces to that of being symmetric, and the conjugate transpose x^* to the usual transpose x'. Note that R(A,cx) = R(A,x) for any real scalar c. Recall that a Hermitian (or real symmetric) matrix has real eigenvalues.

    a. Projection-valued measure
    b. Reality structure
    c. Vectorization
    d. Rayleigh quotient

Chapter 2. DIMENSION, RANK, AND LINEAR TRANSFORMATIONS

20. In geometry, a _____ is a straight curve. When geometry is used to model the real world, lines are used to represent straight objects with negligible width and height. Lines are an idealisation of such objects and have no width or height at all and are usually considered to be infinitely long.

   a. -module
   b. -equivalence
   c. 2-bridge knot
   d. Line

21. In linear algebra, a _____ is a linear transformation that squares to the identity ($R^2 = I$, where R is in K dimensional space), also known as an involution in the general linear group. In addition to reflections across hyperplanes, the class of general reflections includes point reflections, reflections across subspaces of intermediate dimension, and non-orthogonal reflections.

   A _____ over a hyperplane in an inner product space is necessarily symmetric, but a general _____ need not be as the example $\begin{bmatrix} 1 & 0 \\ 1 & -1 \end{bmatrix}$ shows.

   a. Shear mappings
   b. Homomorphic secret sharing
   c. Morphism
   d. Reflection

22. In mathematics, an _____ of a product of sums expresses it as a sum of products by using the fact that multiplication distributes over addition. Expansions of polynomials are obtained by multiplying together their factors, which results in a sum of terms with variables raised to different degrees.

   To multiply two factors, each term of the first factor must be multiplied by each term of the other factor.

   a. Equipotential surfaces
   b. Expansion
   c. Ordered vector space
   d. Analytic subgroup

23. In geometry and trigonometry, an _____ is the figure formed by two rays sharing a common endpoint, called the vertex of the _____ . The magnitude of the _____ is the 'amount of rotation' that separates the two rays, and can be measured by considering the length of circular arc swept out when one ray is rotated about the vertex to coincide with the other Where there is no possibility of confusion, the term '_____' is used interchangeably for both the geometric configuration itself and for its angular magnitude (which is simply a numerical quantity.)

a. ADE classification
b. Angle
c. Abelian P-root group
d. AKS primality test

24. In mathematics, the _____ is an operation which takes two vectors over the real numbers R and returns a real-valued scalar quantity. It is the standard inner product of the orthonormal Euclidean space. It contrasts with the cross product which produces a vector result.
   a. Centrosymmetric matrix
   b. Complex structure
   c. Dot product
   d. Coefficient matrix

25. In abstract algebra, the _____ of a module is a measure of the module's 'size'. It is defined as the _____ of the longest ascending chain of submodules and is a generalization of the concept of dimension for vector spaces. The modules with finite _____ share many important properties with finite-dimensional vector spaces.
   a. Length
   b. Morita equivalence
   c. Supermodule
   d. Finitely generated module

26. _____ is the mathematical process of putting things together. The plus sign '+' means that numbers are added together. For example, in the picture on the right, there are 3 + 2 apples--meaning three apples and two other apples--which is the same as five apples, since 3 + 2 = 5.
   a. Abelian P-root group
   b. AKS primality test
   c. ADE classification
   d. Addition

27. In mathematics, the _____ of a ring R, often denoted char(R), is defined to be the smallest number of times one must add the ring's multiplicative identity element (1) to itself to get the additive identity element (0); the ring is said to have _____ zero if this repeated sum never reaches the additive identity. That is, char(R) is the smallest positive number n such that

$$\underbrace{1 + \cdots + 1}_{n \text{ summands}} = 0$$

Chapter 2. DIMENSION, RANK, AND LINEAR TRANSFORMATIONS 35

if such a number n exists, and 0 otherwise. The _____ may also be taken to be the exponent of the ring's additive group, that is, the smallest positive n such that

$$\underbrace{a + \cdots + a}_{n \text{ summands}} = 0$$

for every element a of the ring (again, if n exists; otherwise zero.)

a. Coherent ring
b. Hereditary
c. Free ideal ring
d. Characteristic

28. In mathematics, a _____ that describes a line D is any vector

$$\overrightarrow{AB}$$

where A and B are two distinct points on the line D. If v is a _____ for D, so is kv for any nonzero scalar k; and these are in fact all of the direction vectors for the line D. Under some definitions, the _____ is required to be a unit vector, in which case each line has exactly two direction vectors, which are negatives of each other (equal in magnitude, opposite in direction.)

Any line in two-dimensional Euclidean space can be described as the set of solutions to an equation of the form

ax + by + c = 0

where a, b, c are real numbers. Then one _____ of (D) is (− b,a).

a. Toeplitz matrix
b. Dual spaces
c. Trace
d. Direction vector

29. In geometry, a _____ is a part of a line that is bounded by two end points, and contains every point on the line between its end points. Examples of line segments include the sides of a triangle or square. More generally, when the end points are both vertices of a polygon, the _____ is either an edge (of that polygon) if they are adjacent vertices, or otherwise a diagonal.

Chapter 2. DIMENSION, RANK, AND LINEAR TRANSFORMATIONS

   a. -module
   b. Skew lines
   c. -equivalence
   d. Line segment

30. In mathematics, the _____ are the following sequence of numbers:

The first two _____ are 0 and 1, and each remaining number is the sum of the previous two:

Some sources omit the initial 0, instead beginning the sequence with two 1s.

In mathematical terms, the sequence F_n of _____ is defined by the recurrence relation

with seed values

   a. Fibonacci numbers
   b. -equivalence
   c. 2-bridge knot
   d. -module

31. In geometry, a _____ is a subset of n-dimensional space that is congruent to a Euclidean space of lower dimension. The flats in two-dimensional space are points and lines, and the flats in three-dimensional space are points, lines, and planes. In n-dimensional space, there are flats of every dimension from 0 to n - 1.
   a. Flat
   b. -module
   c. Similarity
   d. -equivalence

Chapter 2. DIMENSION, RANK, AND LINEAR TRANSFORMATIONS   37

32.   A _____ is a concept in geometry. It is a higher-dimensional generalization of the concepts of a line in the plane and a plane in 3-dimensional space. The most familiar kinds of _____ are affine and linear hyperplanes; less familiar is the projective _____.
  a. Polar homology
  b. Kodaira embedding theorem
  c. Cusp
  d. Hyperplane

Chapter 3. VECTOR SPACES

1. In its simplest meaning in mathematics and logic, an _____ is an action or procedure which produces a new value from one or more input values. There are two common types of operations: unary and binary. Unary operations involve only one value, such as negation and trigonometric functions.
   a. Operation
   b. ADE classification
   c. Abelian P-root group
   d. AKS primality test

2. In linear algebra, a _____ or row matrix is a 1 × n matrix, that is, a matrix consisting of a single row:

$$\mathbf{x} = \begin{bmatrix} x_1 & x_2 & \ldots & x_m \end{bmatrix}.$$

The transpose of a _____ is a column vector:

$$\begin{bmatrix} x_1 \\ x_2 \\ \vdots \\ x_m \end{bmatrix} = \begin{bmatrix} x_1 & x_2 & \ldots & x_m \end{bmatrix}^{\mathrm{T}}.$$

The set of all row vectors forms a vector space which is the dual space to the set of all column vectors.

Row vectors are sometimes written using the following non-standard notation:

$$\mathbf{x} = \begin{bmatrix} x_1, x_2, \ldots, x_m \end{bmatrix}.$$

- Matrix multiplication involves the action of multiplying each _____ of one matrix by each column vector of another matrix.

- The dot product of two vectors a and b is equivalent to multiplying the _____ representation of a by the column vector representation of b:

$$\mathbf{a} \cdot \mathbf{b} = \begin{bmatrix} a_1 & a_2 & a_3 \end{bmatrix} \begin{bmatrix} b_1 \\ b_2 \\ b_3 \end{bmatrix}.$$

Chapter 3. VECTOR SPACES

a. Dual number
b. Dual spaces
c. Polynomial basis
d. Row vector

3. The real component of a quaternion is also called its _____ part.

The term is also sometimes used informally to mean a vector, matrix, tensor, or other usually 'compound' value that is actually reduced to a single component. Thus, for example, the product of a 1×n matrix and an n×1 matrix, which is formally a 1×1 matrix, is often said to be a _____.

a. Tensor product
b. Scalar
c. Self-adjoint
d. Distributivity

4. In mathematics, _____ is one of the basic operations defining a vector space in linear algebra Note that _____ is different from scalar product which is an inner product between two vectors.

More specifically, if K is a field and V is a vector space over K, then _____ is a function from K × V to V. The result of applying this function to c in K and v in V is denoted cv.

a. Scalar multiplication
b. Symplectic vector space
c. K-frame
d. Matrix pencil

5. _____ is the mathematical process of putting things together. The plus sign '+' means that numbers are added together. For example, in the picture on the right, there are 3 + 2 apples--meaning three apples and two other apples--which is the same as five apples, since 3 + 2 = 5.

a. ADE classification
b. Addition
c. Abelian P-root group
d. AKS primality test

6. In mathematics, the _____ are the following sequence of numbers:

Chapter 3. VECTOR SPACES

The first two _____ are 0 and 1, and each remaining number is the sum of the previous two:

Some sources omit the initial 0, instead beginning the sequence with two 1s.

In mathematical terms, the sequence F_n of _____ is defined by the recurrence relation

with seed values

a. -equivalence
b. -module
c. Fibonacci numbers
d. 2-bridge knot

7. In mathematics, a _____ is a constant multiplicative factor of a certain object. For example, in the expression $9x^2$, the _____ of x^2 is 9.

The object can be such things as a variable, a vector, a function, etc.

a. Vandermonde polynomial
b. Tschirnhaus transformation
c. Coefficient
d. Constant term

8. In mathematics, _____ are a concept central to linear algebra and related fields of mathematics

Suppose that K is a field and V is a vector space over K. As usual, we call elements of V vectors and call elements of K scalars.

a. Hyperstructures
b. Groupoid
c. Left alternative
d. Linear combinations

9. In mathematics, for a given complex Hermitian matrix A and nonzero vector x, the _____ R(A,x) is defined as:

$$\frac{x^* A x}{x^* x}.$$

For real matrices and vectors, the condition of being Hermitian reduces to that of being symmetric, and the conjugate transpose x* to the usual transpose x'. Note that R(A,cx) = R(A,x) for any real scalar c. Recall that a Hermitian (or real symmetric) matrix has real eigenvalues.

a. Reality structure
b. Rayleigh quotient
c. Projection-valued measure
d. Vectorization

10. In mathematics, the _____ of a ring R, often denoted char(R), is defined to be the smallest number of times one must add the ring's multiplicative identity element (1) to itself to get the additive identity element (0); the ring is said to have _____ zero if this repeated sum never reaches the additive identity. That is, char(R) is the smallest positive number n such that

$$\underbrace{1 + \cdots + 1}_{n \text{ summands}} = 0$$

if such a number n exists, and 0 otherwise. The _____ may also be taken to be the exponent of the ring's additive group, that is, the smallest positive n such that

$$\underbrace{a + \cdots + a}_{n \text{ summands}} = 0$$

for every element a of the ring (again, if n exists; otherwise zero.)

a. Hereditary
b. Coherent ring
c. Free ideal ring
d. Characteristic

11. In linear algebra, the _____ or unit matrix of size n is the n-by-n square matrix with ones on the main diagonal and zeros elsewhere. It is denoted by I_n, or simply by I if the size is immaterial or can be trivially determined by the context. (In some fields, such as quantum mechanics, the _____ is denoted by a boldface one, 1; otherwise it is identical to I.)
a. Associativity
b. Orthogonal
c. Artinian ideal
d. Identity matrix

12. In linear algebra, a family of vectors is _____ if none of them can be written as a linear combination of finitely many other vectors in the collection. A family of vectors which is not _____ is called linearly dependent. For instance, in the three-dimensional real vector space $\mathbb{R}^3$ we have the following example.
a. Composition ring
b. Derivative algebra
c. Grothendieck group
d. Linearly independent

13. In mathematics, a _____ is a rectangular array of numbers. This way, matrices can record data that depend on multiple parameters. In particular they are used to keep track of the coefficients of multiple linear equations. Matrices are closely connected to linear transformations, which are higher-dimensional analogs of linear functions, i.e., functions of the form f(x) = c · x, where c is a constant. This map corresponds to a _____ with one row and column, with entry c. In addition to a number of elementary, entrywise operations such as _____ addition a key notion is _____ multiplication, which displays a number of features not encountered in numbers; for example, products of matrices depend on the order of the factors, unlike products of real numbers, say, where c · d = d · c for any two numbers c and d.
a. Polynomial expression
b. Heap
c. Commutativity
d. Matrix

14. In linear algebra, a _____ is a set of vectors that, in a linear combination, can represent every vector in a given vector space or free module, and such that no element of the set can be represented as a linear combination of the others. In other words, a _____ is a linearly independent spanning set.

a. Chirality
b. Supergroup
c. Minor
d. Basis

15. In linear algebra, a square matrix A is called diagonalizable if it is similar to a diagonal matrix, i.e., if there exists an invertible matrix P such that P $^{-1}$AP is a diagonal matrix. If V is a finite-dimensional vector space, then a linear map T : V → V is called diagonalizable if there exists a basis of V with respect to which T is represented by a diagonal matrix. Diagonalization is the process of finding a corresponding diagonal matrix for a _____ or linear map.
   a. Hamiltonian matrix
   b. Diagonalizable matrix
   c. Pascal matrix
   d. Cauchy matrix

16. In mathematics, the _____ of a vector space V is the cardinality (i.e. the number of vectors) of a basis of V. It is sometimes called Hamel _____ or algebraic _____ to distinguish it from other types of _____. All bases of a vector space have equal cardinality and so the _____ of a vector space is uniquely defined. The _____ of the vector space V over the field F can be written as dim$_F$(V) or as [V : F], read '_____ of V over F'.
   a. Dual basis
   b. Dimension
   c. Partial trace
   d. Cofactor

17. In linear algebra, a _____ or column matrix is an m × 1 matrix, i.e. a matrix consisting of a single column of m elements.

$$\mathbf{x} = \begin{bmatrix} x_1 \\ x_2 \\ \vdots \\ x_m \end{bmatrix}$$

The transpose of a _____ is a row vector and vice versa.

The set of all column vectors forms a vector space which is the dual space to the set of all row vectors.

a. K-frame
b. Symplectic vector space
c. Normal basis
d. Column vector

18. In linear algebra, a _____ is an explicit representation of a vector in an abstract vector space as an ordered list of numbers or, equivalently, as an element of the coordinate space F^n. Coordinate vectors allow calculations with abstract objects to be transformed into calculations with blocks of numbers (matrices and column vectors.)

Let V be a vector space of dimension n over a field F and let

$$B = \{b_1, b_2, \ldots, b_n\}$$

be an ordered basis for V. Then for every $v \in V$ there is a unique linear combination of the basis vectors that equals v:

$$v = \alpha_1 b_1 + \alpha_2 b_2 + \cdots + \alpha_n b_n$$

$$v_B = (\alpha_1, \alpha_2, \cdots, \alpha_n)$$

This is also called the representation of v with respect of B, or the B representation of v.

a. Homogeneous coordinates
b. Direction vector
c. Coordinate vector
d. Cofactor

19. In mathematics, a _____ represents the application of one function to the results of another. For instance, the functions f: X → Y and g: Y → Z can be composed by first computing f(x) and then applying a function g to the output of f(x).

Thus one obtains a function g ∘ f: X → Z defined by (g ∘ f)(x) = g(f(x)) for all x in X. The notation g ∘ f is read as 'g circle f', or 'g composed with f', 'g after f', 'g following f', or just 'g of f'.

a. Shear mappings
b. Composite function
c. Reflection
d. Linear map

Chapter 3. VECTOR SPACES

20. In mathematics, especially in the area of abstract algebra known as ring theory, a _____ is a ring with 0 ≠ 1 such that ab = 0 implies that either a = 0 or b = 0 (the zero-product property.) That is, it is a nontrivial ring without left or right zero divisors. A commutative _____ is called an integral _____.
    a. Coherent ring
    b. Subring
    c. Partially-ordered ring
    d. Domain

21. A _____ is a mathematical equation for an unknown function of one or several variables that relates the values of the function itself and its derivatives of various orders. Differential equations play a prominent role in engineering, physics, economics and other disciplines. Visualization of airflow into a duct modelled using the Navier-Stokes equations, a set of partial differential equations.

    Differential equations arise in many areas of science and technology; whenever a deterministic relationship involving some continuously changing quantities (modeled by functions) and their rates of change (expressed as derivatives) is known or postulated.

    a. Differential equation
    b. -equivalence
    c. 2-bridge knot
    d. -module

22. In the various branches of mathematics that fall under the heading of abstract algebra, the _____ of a homomorphism measures the degree to which the homomorphism fails to be injective. An important special case is the _____ of a matrix, also called the null space.

    The definition of _____ takes various forms in various contexts.

    a. K-theory
    b. Monomial basis
    c. Kernel
    d. Completing the square

23. Let S be a set with a binary operation * . If e is an identity element of (S, *) and a * b = e, then a is called a _____ of b and b is called a right inverse of a. If an element x is both a _____ and a right inverse of y, then x is called a two-sided inverse, or simply an inverse, of y.

a. 2-bridge knot
b. -equivalence
c. -module
d. Left inverse

24. In abstract algebra, an _____ is a bijective map f such that both f and its inverse f^{-1} are homomorphisms, i.e., structure-preserving mappings. In the more general setting of category theory, an _____ is a morphism f:X→Y in a category for which there exists an 'inverse' f^{-1}:Y→X, with the property that both $f^{-1}f=id_X$ and $ff^{-1}=id_Y$.

Informally, an _____ is a kind of mapping between objects, which shows a relationship between two properties or operations.

a. Epimorphism
b. Endomorphism
c. ADE classification
d. Isomorphism

25. A _____ is a method used by a computer language to store matrices of more than one dimension in memory.

Fortran and C use different schemes. Fortran uses 'Column Major', in which all the elements for a given column are stored contiguously in memory.

a. Skew-Hermitian matrix
b. Polynomial matrix
c. Moment matrix
d. Matrix representation

26. In linear algebra, functional analysis and related areas of mathematics, a _____ is a function that assigns a strictly positive length or size to all vectors in a vector space, other than the zero vector. A seminorm (or pseudonorm), on the other hand, is allowed to assign zero length to some non-zero vectors.

A simple example is the 2-dimensional Euclidean space R^2 equipped with the Euclidean _____.

a. -module
b. Quasinorm
c. Norm
d. -equivalence

Chapter 3. VECTOR SPACES

27. In mathematics, the Cauchy-_____ the Cauchy inequality is a useful inequality encountered in many different settings, such as linear algebra applied to vectors, in analysis applied to infinite series and integration of products, and in probability theory, applied to variances and covariances. The general formulation of the Heisenberg uncertainty principle is derived using the Cauchy-_____ in the Hilbert space of pure quantum states.

The inequality for sums was published by , while the corresponding inequality for integrals was first stated by and rediscovered by

   a. 2-bridge knot
   b. Schwarz inequality
   c. -equivalence
   d. -module

28. In mathematics, an _____ is a statement about the relative size or order of two objects, or about whether they are the same or not

   - The notation a < b means that a is less than b.
   - The notation a > b means that a is greater than b.
   - The notation a ≠ b means that a is not equal to b, but does not say that one is bigger than the other or even that they can be compared in size.

In all these cases, a is not equal to b, hence, '_____'.

These relations are known as strict _____

   - The notation a ≤ b means that a is less than or equal to b (or, equivalently, not greater than b);
   - The notation a ≥ b means that a is greater than or equal to b (or, equivalently, not smaller than b);

An additional use of the notation is to show that one quantity is much greater than another, normally by several orders of magnitude.

   - The notation a ≪ b means that a is much less than b.
   - The notation a ≫ b means that a is much greater than b.

If the sense of the _____ is the same for all values of the variables for which its members are defined, then the _____ is called an 'absolute' or 'unconditional' _____. If the sense of an _____ holds only for certain values of the variables involved, but is reversed or destroyed for other values of the variables, it is called a conditional _____.

One can apply the same algebraic operations to inequalities as one would apply for solving equalities. For example, to find x for the _____ 10x > 20 one would divide 20 by 10 to obtain x > 2.

a. Abelian P-root group
b. ADE classification
c. AKS primality test
d. Inequality

29. In linear algebra, the _____ of a matrix A is another matrix A^T (also written A', A^{tr} or ^tA) created by any one of the following equivalent actions:

- write the rows of A as the columns of A^T
- write the columns of A as the rows of A^T
- reflect A by its main diagonal (which starts from the top left) to obtain A^T

Formally, the _____ of an m × n matrix A with elements A_{ij} is the n × m matrix

$$A^T_{ij} = A_{ji} \text{ for } 1 \leq i \leq n, 1 \leq j \leq m.$$

The _____ of a scalar is the same scalar.

- $\begin{bmatrix} 1 & 2 \end{bmatrix}^T = \begin{bmatrix} 1 \\ 2 \end{bmatrix}.$

- $\begin{bmatrix} 1 & 2 \\ 3 & 4 \end{bmatrix}^T = \begin{bmatrix} 1 & 3 \\ 2 & 4 \end{bmatrix}.$

- $\begin{bmatrix} 1 & 2 \\ 3 & 4 \\ 5 & 6 \end{bmatrix}^T = \begin{bmatrix} 1 & 3 & 5 \\ 2 & 4 & 6 \end{bmatrix}.$

For matrices A, B and scalar c we have the following properties of _____:

1. $\left(\mathbf{A}^T\right)^T = \mathbf{A}$

    Taking the _____ is an involution (self inverse.)

- $(\mathbf{A} + \mathbf{B})^T = \mathbf{A}^T + \mathbf{B}^T$

The _____ respects addition.

- $(\mathbf{AB})^\mathrm{T} = \mathbf{B}^\mathrm{T}\mathbf{A}^\mathrm{T}$

    Note that the order of the factors reverses. From this one can deduce that a square matrix A is invertible if and only if A^T is invertible, and in this case we have $(A^{-1})^T = (A^T)^{-1}$. It is relatively easy to extend this result to the general case of multiple matrices, where we find that $(ABC...XYZ)^T = Z^T Y^T X^T ... C^T B^T A^T$.

- $(c\mathbf{A})^\mathrm{T} = c\mathbf{A}^\mathrm{T}$

    The _____ of a scalar is the same scalar. Together with (2), this states that the _____ is a linear map from the space of m × n matrices to the space of all n × m matrices.

- $\det(\mathbf{A}^\mathrm{T}) = \det(\mathbf{A})$

    The determinant of a square matrix is the same as that of its _____.

- The dot product of two column vectors a and b can be computed as

$$\mathbf{a} \cdot \mathbf{b} = \mathbf{a}^\mathrm{T}\mathbf{b},$$

which is written as $a_i\, b^i$ in Einstein notation.
- If A has only real entries, then $A^T A$ is a positive-semidefinite matrix.
- $(\mathbf{A}^\mathrm{T})^{-1} = (\mathbf{A}^{-1})^\mathrm{T}$

    The _____ of an invertible matrix is also invertible, and its inverse is the _____ of the inverse of the original matrix.

- If A is a square matrix, then its eigenvalues are equal to the eigenvalues of its _____.

A square matrix whose _____ is equal to itself is called a symmetric matrix; that is, A is symmetric if

$$\mathbf{A}^\mathrm{T} = \mathbf{A}.$$

A square matrix whose _____ is also its inverse is called an orthogonal matrix; that is, G is orthogonal if

$$\mathbf{G}\mathbf{G}^\mathrm{T} = \mathbf{G}^\mathrm{T}\mathbf{G} = \mathbf{I}_n,$$ the identity matrix, i.e. $G^T = G^{-1}$.

Chapter 3. VECTOR SPACES

A square matrix whose _____ is equal to its negative is called skew-symmetric matrix; that is, A is skew-symmetric if

$$\mathbf{A}^T = -\mathbf{A}.$$

The conjugate _____ of the complex matrix A, written as A*, is obtained by taking the _____ of A and the complex conjugate of each entry:

$$\mathbf{A}^* = (\overline{\mathbf{A}})^T = \overline{(\mathbf{A}^T)}.$$

If f: V→W is a linear map between vector spaces V and W with nondegenerate bilinear forms, we define the _____ of f to be the linear map $^t f$: W→V, determined by

$$B_V(v, {}^t f(w)) = B_W(f(v), w) \quad \forall\, v \in V, w \in W.$$

Here, B_V and B_W are the bilinear forms on V and W respectively. The matrix of the _____ of a map is the transposed matrix only if the bases are orthonormal with respect to their bilinear forms.

Over a complex vector space, one often works with sesquilinear forms instead of bilinear (conjugate-linear in one argument.)

   a. Levinson recursion
   b. Drazin inverse
   c. Tridiagonal matrix
   d. Transpose

30. A _____ is one of the basic shapes of geometry: a polygon with three corners or vertices and three sides or edges which are line segments. A _____ with vertices A, B, and C is denoted ABC.

In Euclidean geometry any three non-collinear points determine a unique _____ and a unique plane (i.e. a two-dimensional Euclidean space.)

   a. 2-bridge knot
   b. -module
   c. Triangle
   d. -equivalence

Chapter 3. VECTOR SPACES

31. In mathematics, the _____ states that for any triangle, the length of a given side must be less than the sum of the other two sides but greater than the difference between the two sides.

In Euclidean geometry and some other geometries this is a theorem. In the Euclidean case, in both the less than or equal to and greater than or equal to statements, equality occurs only if the triangle has a 180° angle and two 0° angles, as shown in the bottom example in the image to the right.

a. -equivalence
b. -module
c. 2-bridge knot
d. Triangle inequality

32. The a-_____ of a string, for a a letter, is the number of times that letter occurs in the string. More precisely, let A be a finite set (called the alphabet), $a \in A$ a letter of A, and $c \in A^*$ a string (where A* is the free monoid generated by the elements of A, equivalently the set of strings, including the empty string, whose letters are from A.) Then the a-_____ of c, denoted by $wt_a(c)$, is the number of times the generator a occurs in the unique expression for c as a product (concatenation) of letters in A.

a. Presentation of a monoid
b. Trace monoid
c. Biordered set
d. Weight

Chapter 4. DETERMINANTS

1. In algebra, a _____ is a function depending on n that associates a scalar, det(A), to an n×n square matrix A. The fundamental geometric meaning of a _____ is a scale factor for measure when A is regarded as a linear transformation. Determinants are important both in calculus, where they enter the substitution rule for several variables, and in multilinear algebra.

For a fixed nonnegative integer n, there is a unique _____ function for the n×n matrices over any commutative ring R. In particular, this function exists when R is the field of real or complex numbers.

   a. Leibniz formula
   b. Determinant
   c. Functional determinant
   d. Pfaffian

2. In mathematics, the _____ of a ring R, often denoted char(R), is defined to be the smallest number of times one must add the ring's multiplicative identity element (1) to itself to get the additive identity element (0); the ring is said to have _____ zero if this repeated sum never reaches the additive identity. That is, char(R) is the smallest positive number n such that

$$\underbrace{1 + \cdots + 1}_{n \text{ summands}} = 0$$

if such a number n exists, and 0 otherwise. The _____ may also be taken to be the exponent of the ring's additive group, that is, the smallest positive n such that

$$\underbrace{a + \cdots + a}_{n \text{ summands}} = 0$$

for every element a of the ring (again, if n exists; otherwise zero.)

   a. Free ideal ring
   b. Hereditary
   c. Coherent ring
   d. Characteristic

3. In mathematics, the _____ is a binary operation on two vectors in a three-dimensional Euclidean space that results in another vector which is perpendicular to the plane containing the two input vectors. The algebra defined by the _____ is neither commutative nor associative. It contrasts with the dot product which produces a scalar result.

a. Row space
b. Differential graded algebra
c. Formal power series
d. Cross product

4. _____, in mathematics, are a non-commutative number system that extends the complex numbers. The _____ were first described by Irish mathematician Sir William Rowan Hamilton in 1843 and applied to mechanics in three-dimensional space. They find uses in both theoretical and applied mathematics, in particular for calculations involving three-dimensional rotations , such as in 3D computer graphics, although they have been superseded in many applications by vectors and matrices.
   a. Split-quaternions
   b. Generalized quaternion interpolation
   c. Split-biquaternion
   d. Quaternions

5. In mathematics and physics, the _____ is a common mnemonic for understanding notation conventions for vectors in 3 dimensions. It was invented for use in electromagnetism by British physicist Zachariah William Cole in the late 1800s.

When choosing three vectors that must be at right angles to each other, there are two distinct solutions, so when expressing this idea in mathematics, one must remove the ambiguity of which solution is meant.

   a. -equivalence
   b. -module
   c. 2-bridge knot
   d. Right-hand rule

6. In mathematics, a _____ is a rectangular array of numbers. This way, matrices can record data that depend on multiple parameters. In particular they are used to keep track of the coefficients of multiple linear equations. Matrices are closely connected to linear transformations, which are higher-dimensional analogs of linear functions, i.e., functions of the form $f(x) = c · x$, where c is a constant. This map corresponds to a _____ with one row and column, with entry c. In addition to a number of elementary, entrywise operations such as _____ addition a key notion is _____ multiplication, which displays a number of features not encountered in numbers; for example, products of matrices depend on the order of the factors, unlike products of real numbers, say, where $c · d = d · c$ for any two numbers c and d.
   a. Commutativity
   b. Heap
   c. Matrix
   d. Polynomial expression

Chapter 4. DETERMINANTS

7. In linear algebra, a _____ of a matrix A is the determinant of some smaller square matrix, cut down from A by removing one or more of its rows or columns. Minors obtained by removing just one row and one column from square matrices (first minors) are required for calculating matrix cofactors, which in turn are useful for computing both the determinant and inverse of square matrices.
    a. Purification
    b. Supergroup
    c. Rng
    d. Minor

8. In linear algebra, the _____ describes a particular construction that is useful for calculating both the determinant and inverse of square matrices. Specifically the _____ of the (i, j) entry of a matrix, also known as the (i, j) _____ of that matrix, is the signed minor of that entry.

Finding the minors of a matrix A is a multi-step process:

1. Choose an entry a_{ij} from the matrix.
2. Cross out the entries that lie in the corresponding row i and column j.
3. Rewrite the matrix without the marked entries.
4. Obtain the determinant M_{ij} of this new matrix.

M_{ij} is termed the minor for entry a_{ij}.

If i + j is an even number, the _____ C_{ij} of a_{ij} coincides with its minor:

$$C_{ij} = M_{ij}.$$

Otherwise, it is equal to the additive inverse of its minor:

$$C_{ij} = -M_{ij}.$$

If A is a square matrix, then the minor of its entry a_{ij}, also known as the i,j, or (i,j), or (i,j)[th] minor of A, is denoted by M_{ij} and is defined to be the determinant of the submatrix obtained by removing from A its i-th row and j-th column.

   a. Cofactor
   b. Complex structure
   c. Coefficient matrix
   d. Resolvent set

Chapter 4. DETERMINANTS

9. In mathematics, an _____ of a product of sums expresses it as a sum of products by using the fact that multiplication distributes over addition. Expansions of polynomials are obtained by multiplying together their factors, which results in a sum of terms with variables raised to different degrees.

To multiply two factors, each term of the first factor must be multiplied by each term of the other factor.

   a. Analytic subgroup
   b. Equipotential surfaces
   c. Expansion
   d. Ordered vector space

10. In algebraic topology, a simplicial k-_____ is a formal linear combination of k-simplices.

Integration is defined on chains by taking the linear combination of integrals over the simplices in the _____ with coefficients typically integers. The set of all k-chains forms a group and the sequence of these groups is called a _____ complex.

   a. Bockstein homomorphism
   b. Tesseract
   c. Combinatorial topology
   d. Chain

11. _____ is the mathematical process of putting things together. The plus sign '+' means that numbers are added together. For example, in the picture on the right, there are 3 + 2 apples--meaning three apples and two other apples--which is the same as five apples, since 3 + 2 = 5.

   a. Addition
   b. AKS primality test
   c. ADE classification
   d. Abelian P-root group

12. In linear algebra, a square matrix A is called diagonalizable if it is similar to a diagonal matrix, i.e., if there exists an invertible matrix P such that $P^{-1}AP$ is a diagonal matrix. If V is a finite-dimensional vector space, then a linear map $T : V \to V$ is called diagonalizable if there exists a basis of V with respect to which T is represented by a diagonal matrix. Diagonalization is the process of finding a corresponding diagonal matrix for a _____ or linear map.

   a. Diagonalizable matrix
   b. Cauchy matrix
   c. Pascal matrix
   d. Hamiltonian matrix

13. In mathematics, an _____ on a real vector space is a choice of which ordered bases are 'positively' oriented and which are 'negatively' oriented. In the three-dimensional Euclidean space, the two possible basis orientations are called right-handed and left-handed (or right-chiral and left-chiral), respectively. However, the choice of _____ is independent of the handedness or chirality of the bases (although right-handed bases are typically declared to be positively oriented, they may also be assigned a negative _____.)
    a. Orientation
    b. Orthogonal Procrustes problem
    c. Overdetermined
    d. Elementary matrix

Chapter 5. EIGENVALUES AND EIGENVECTORS

1. In mathematics, the _____ are the following sequence of numbers:

    The first two _____ are 0 and 1, and each remaining number is the sum of the previous two:

    Some sources omit the initial 0, instead beginning the sequence with two 1s.

    In mathematical terms, the sequence F_n of _____ is defined by the recurrence relation

    with seed values

    a. 2-bridge knot
    b. -module
    c. Fibonacci numbers
    d. -equivalence

2. In linear algebra, the _____ states that every square matrix over the real or complex field satisfies its own characteristic equation.

    More precisely; if A is the given n×n matrix and I_n is the n×n identity matrix, then the characteristic polynomial of A is defined as:

    where 'det' is the determinant function. The _____ states that substituting the matrix A in the characteristic polynomial (which involves multiplying its constant term by I_n, since that is the zeroth power of A) results in the zero matrix:

    The _____ also holds for square matrices over commutative rings.

a. -module
b. Cayley-Hamilton theorem
c. 2-bridge knot
d. -equivalence

3. In mathematics, the _____ of a ring R, often denoted char(R), is defined to be the smallest number of times one must add the ring's multiplicative identity element (1) to itself to get the additive identity element (0); the ring is said to have _____ zero if this repeated sum never reaches the additive identity. That is, char(R) is the smallest positive number n such that

$$\underbrace{1 + \cdots + 1}_{n \text{ summands}} = 0$$

if such a number n exists, and 0 otherwise. The _____ may also be taken to be the exponent of the ring's additive group, that is, the smallest positive n such that

$$\underbrace{a + \cdots + a}_{n \text{ summands}} = 0$$

for every element a of the ring (again, if n exists; otherwise zero.)

a. Hereditary
b. Free ideal ring
c. Characteristic
d. Coherent ring

4. In linear algebra, a square matrix A is called diagonalizable if it is similar to a diagonal matrix, i.e., if there exists an invertible matrix P such that $P^{-1}AP$ is a diagonal matrix. If V is a finite-dimensional vector space, then a linear map $T : V \to V$ is called diagonalizable if there exists a basis of V with respect to which T is represented by a diagonal matrix. Diagonalization is the process of finding a corresponding diagonal matrix for a _____ or linear map.

a. Cauchy matrix
b. Pascal matrix
c. Hamiltonian matrix
d. Diagonalizable matrix

5. For each eigenvector of a linear transformation, there is a corresponding scalar value called an _____ for that vector, which determines the amount the eigenvector is scaled under the linear transformation. For example, an _____ of +2 means that the eigenvector is doubled in length and points in the same direction. An _____ of +1 means that the eigenvector is unchanged, while an _____ of −1 means that the eigenvector is reversed in sense.

Chapter 5. EIGENVALUES AND EIGENVECTORS

a. Abelian P-root group
b. ADE classification
c. AKS primality test
d. Eigenvalue

6. For each _____ of a linear transformation, there is a corresponding scalar value called an eigenvalue for that vector, which determines the amount the _____ is scaled under the linear transformation. For example, an eigenvalue of +2 means that the _____ is doubled in length and points in the same direction. An eigenvalue of +1 means that the _____ is unchanged, while an eigenvalue of −1 means that the _____ is reversed in sense.
   a. Eigenvector
   b. Abelian P-root group
   c. ADE classification
   d. AKS primality test

7. In linear algebra, the _____ or unit matrix of size n is the n-by-n square matrix with ones on the main diagonal and zeros elsewhere. It is denoted by I_n, or simply by I if the size is immaterial or can be trivially determined by the context. (In some fields, such as quantum mechanics, the _____ is denoted by a boldface one, 1; otherwise it is identical to I.)
   a. Orthogonal
   b. Associativity
   c. Artinian ideal
   d. Identity matrix

8. In mathematics, a _____ is a rectangular array of numbers. This way, matrices can record data that depend on multiple parameters. In particular they are used to keep track of the coefficients of multiple linear equations. Matrices are closely connected to linear transformations, which are higher-dimensional analogs of linear functions, i.e., functions of the form f(x) = c Â· x, where c is a constant. This map corresponds to a _____ with one row and column, with entry c. In addition to a number of elementary, entrywise operations such as _____ addition a key notion is _____ multiplication, which displays a number of features not encountered in numbers; for example, products of matrices depend on the order of the factors, unlike products of real numbers, say, where c Â· d = d Â· c for any two numbers c and d.
   a. Heap
   b. Polynomial expression
   c. Commutativity
   d. Matrix

Chapter 5. EIGENVALUES AND EIGENVECTORS

9. In linear algebra, the _____ of a matrix A is another matrix A^T (also written A', A^{tr} or ^tA) created by any one of the following equivalent actions:

- write the rows of A as the columns of A^T
- write the columns of A as the rows of A^T
- reflect A by its main diagonal (which starts from the top left) to obtain A^T

Formally, the _____ of an m × n matrix A with elements A_{ij} is the n × m matrix

$$A^T_{ij} = A_{ji} \text{ for } 1 \leq i \leq n, 1 \leq j \leq m.$$

The _____ of a scalar is the same scalar.

- $\begin{bmatrix} 1 & 2 \end{bmatrix}^T = \begin{bmatrix} 1 \\ 2 \end{bmatrix}.$

- $\begin{bmatrix} 1 & 2 \\ 3 & 4 \end{bmatrix}^T = \begin{bmatrix} 1 & 3 \\ 2 & 4 \end{bmatrix}.$

- $\begin{bmatrix} 1 & 2 \\ 3 & 4 \\ 5 & 6 \end{bmatrix}^T = \begin{bmatrix} 1 & 3 & 5 \\ 2 & 4 & 6 \end{bmatrix}.$

For matrices A, B and scalar c we have the following properties of _____:

1. $\left(A^T\right)^T = A$

    Taking the _____ is an involution (self inverse.)

- $(A + B)^T = A^T + B^T$

    The _____ respects addition.

- $(AB)^T = B^T A^T$

Chapter 5. EIGENVALUES AND EIGENVECTORS

Note that the order of the factors reverses. From this one can deduce that a square matrix A is invertible if and only if A^T is invertible, and in this case we have $(A^{-1})^T = (A^T)^{-1}$. It is relatively easy to extend this result to the general case of multiple matrices, where we find that $(ABC...XYZ)^T = Z^T Y^T X^T ... C^T B^T A^T$.

- $(c\mathbf{A})^T = c\mathbf{A}^T$

  The _____ of a scalar is the same scalar. Together with (2), this states that the _____ is a linear map from the space of m × n matrices to the space of all n × m matrices.

- $\det(\mathbf{A}^T) = \det(\mathbf{A})$

  The determinant of a square matrix is the same as that of its _____.

- The dot product of two column vectors a and b can be computed as

  $$\mathbf{a} \cdot \mathbf{b} = \mathbf{a}^T \mathbf{b},$$

which is written as $a_i b^i$ in Einstein notation.
- If A has only real entries, then $A^T A$ is a positive-semidefinite matrix.
- $(\mathbf{A}^T)^{-1} = (\mathbf{A}^{-1})^T$

  The _____ of an invertible matrix is also invertible, and its inverse is the _____ of the inverse of the original matrix.

- If A is a square matrix, then its eigenvalues are equal to the eigenvalues of its _____.

A square matrix whose _____ is equal to itself is called a symmetric matrix; that is, A is symmetric if

$$\mathbf{A}^T = \mathbf{A}.$$

A square matrix whose _____ is also its inverse is called an orthogonal matrix; that is, G is orthogonal if

$$\mathbf{G}\mathbf{G}^T = \mathbf{G}^T \mathbf{G} = \mathbf{I}_n,$$ the identity matrix, i.e. $G^T = G^{-1}$.

A square matrix whose _____ is equal to its negative is called skew-symmetric matrix; that is, A is skew-symmetric if

$$\mathbf{A}^T = -\mathbf{A}.$$

Chapter 5. EIGENVALUES AND EIGENVECTORS

The conjugate _____ of the complex matrix A, written as A*, is obtained by taking the _____ of A and the complex conjugate of each entry:

$$\mathbf{A}^* = (\overline{\mathbf{A}})^{\mathrm{T}} = \overline{(\mathbf{A}^{\mathrm{T}})}.$$

If f: V→W is a linear map between vector spaces V and W with nondegenerate bilinear forms, we define the _____ of f to be the linear map ${}^t f : W \to V$, determined by

$$B_V(v, {}^t f(w)) = B_W(f(v), w) \quad \forall\, v \in V, w \in W.$$

Here, B_V and B_W are the bilinear forms on V and W respectively. The matrix of the _____ of a map is the transposed matrix only if the bases are orthonormal with respect to their bilinear forms.

Over a complex vector space, one often works with sesquilinear forms instead of bilinear (conjugate-linear in one argument.)

a. Levinson recursion
b. Tridiagonal matrix
c. Transpose
d. Drazin inverse

10. In algebraic topology, a simplicial k-_____ is a formal linear combination of k-simplices.

Integration is defined on chains by taking the linear combination of integrals over the simplices in the _____ with coefficients typically integers. The set of all k-chains forms a group and the sequence of these groups is called a _____ complex.

a. Chain
b. Bockstein homomorphism
c. Tesseract
d. Combinatorial topology

11. In discrete mathematics, the _____ is used when solving recurrence problems. One can specify a recurrence relation of the form

$$t_n = At_{n-1} + Bt_{n-2}$$

where the value of t_n is dependent on the values of t_{n-1} and t_{n-2}. When solving a recurrence relation, the goal is to eliminate this dependency and derive an equation of the form

$$t_n = c_1 r_1^n + c_2 r_2^n,$$

where c_1 and c_2 are constants and r_1 and r_2 are the roots of the _____

$$r^2 - Ar - B = 0,$$

where A and B are the constants defined in the original recurrence relation.

a. Characteristic equation
b. -equivalence
c. -module
d. 2-bridge knot

12. In linear algebra, one associates a polynomial to every square matrix, its _____. This polynomial encodes several important properties of the matrix, most notably its eigenvalues, its determinant and its trace.

Given a square matrix A, we want to find a polynomial whose roots are precisely the eigenvalues of A. For a diagonal matrix A, the _____ is easy to define: if the diagonal entries are a_1, a_2, a_3, etc.

a. Square-free polynomial
b. Characteristic polynomial
c. Quasi-polynomial
d. Constant term

13. In mathematics, _____ are a concept central to linear algebra and related fields of mathematics

Suppose that K is a field and V is a vector space over K. As usual, we call elements of V vectors and call elements of K scalars.

a. Groupoid
b. Left alternative
c. Hyperstructures
d. Linear combinations

14. In mathematics, a _____ is a function between two vector spaces that preserves the operations of vector addition and scalar multiplication. The expression 'linear operator' is in especially common use, for linear maps from a vector space to itself In advanced mathematics, the definition of linear function coincides with the definition of _____.

   a. Rotation
   b. Linear map
   c. Homomorphic secret sharing
   d. Real matrices

15. Generally, in mathematics, a _____ of an object is a standard way of presenting that object.

_____ can also mean a differential form that is defined in a natural (canonical) way; see below.

Suppose we have some set S of objects, with an equivalence relation.

   a. Monomial basis
   b. Cylindrical algebraic decomposition
   c. Canonical form
   d. Brahmagupta's identity

16. In linear algebra, the _____ of an n-by-n square matrix A is defined to be the sum of the elements on the main diagonal (the diagonal from the upper left to the lower right) of A, i.e.,

$$\operatorname{tr}(A) = a_{11} + a_{22} + \cdots + a_{nn} = \sum_{i=1}^{n} a_{ii}$$

where a_{ij} represents the entry on the ith row and jth column of A. Equivalently, the _____ of a matrix is the sum of its eigenvalues, making it an invariant with respect to a change of basis. This characterization can be used to define the _____ for a linear operator in general.

Note that the _____ is only defined for a square matrix (i.e. n×n.)

   a. Coefficient matrix
   b. Dot product
   c. Defective matrix
   d. Trace

17. In linear algebra, two n-by-n matrices A and B are called _____ if

Chapter 5. EIGENVALUES AND EIGENVECTORS

$$B = P^{-1}AP$$

for some invertible n-by-n matrix P. _____ matrices represent the same linear transformation under two different bases, with P being the change of basis matrix.

The matrix P is sometimes called a similarity transformation. In the context of matrix groups, similarity is sometimes referred to as conjugacy, with _____ matrices being conjugate.

a. Zero matrix
b. Skew-symmetric
c. Similar
d. Cartan matrix

18. In mathematics, for a given complex Hermitian matrix A and nonzero vector x, the _____ R(A,x) is defined as:

$$\frac{x^* A x}{x^* x}.$$

For real matrices and vectors, the condition of being Hermitian reduces to that of being symmetric, and the conjugate transpose x* to the usual transpose x'. Note that R(A,cx) = R(A,x) for any real scalar c. Recall that a Hermitian (or real symmetric) matrix has real eigenvalues.

a. Vectorization
b. Projection-valued measure
c. Reality structure
d. Rayleigh quotient

19. In linear algebra, a _____ matrix is a matrix that is 'almost' a diagonal matrix. To be exact: a _____ matrix has nonzero elements only in the main diagonal, the first diagonal below this, and the first diagonal above the main diagonal.

For example, the following matrix is _____:

$$\begin{pmatrix} 1 & 4 & 0 & 0 \\ 3 & 4 & 1 & 0 \\ 0 & 2 & 3 & 4 \\ 0 & 0 & 1 & 3 \end{pmatrix}.$$

A determinant formed from a _____ matrix is known as a continuant.

a. -module
b. Tridiagonal
c. -equivalence
d. 2-bridge knot

20. In linear algebra, a _____ is a matrix that is 'almost' a diagonal matrix. To be exact: a _____ has nonzero elements only in the main diagonal, the first diagonal below this, and the first diagonal above the main diagonal.

For example, the following matrix is tridiagonal:

$$\begin{pmatrix} 1 & 4 & 0 & 0 \\ 3 & 4 & 1 & 0 \\ 0 & 2 & 3 & 4 \\ 0 & 0 & 1 & 3 \end{pmatrix}.$$

A determinant formed from a _____ is known as a continuant.

a. Diagonalizable matrix
b. Similar
c. Wilkinson matrices
d. Tridiagonal matrix

21. A _____ is a mathematical equation for an unknown function of one or several variables that relates the values of the function itself and its derivatives of various orders. Differential equations play a prominent role in engineering, physics, economics and other disciplines. Visualization of airflow into a duct modelled using the Navier-Stokes equations, a set of partial differential equations.

Differential equations arise in many areas of science and technology; whenever a deterministic relationship involving some continuously changing quantities (modeled by functions) and their rates of change (expressed as derivatives) is known or postulated.

a. 2-bridge knot
b. -equivalence
c. -module
d. Differential equation

Chapter 6. ORTHOGONALITY

1. In linear algebra and functional analysis, a _____ is a linear transformation P from a vector space to itself such that $P^2 = P$. It leaves its image unchanged. Though abstract, this definition of '_____' formalizes and generalizes the idea of graphical _____.
   a. Lumer-Phillips theorem
   b. C_0-semigroup
   c. Convolution power
   d. Projection

2. In discrete mathematics and predominantly in set theory, a _____ is a concept used in comparisons of sets to refer to the unique values of one set in relation to another. The terms 'absolute' and 'relative' _____ refer to more specific applications of the concept, with universal complements referring to elements unique to the universal set and the latter referring to the unique elements of one set in relation to another. In this image, the universal set is represented by the border of the image, and the set A as a disc.
   a. -module
   b. Pointed set
   c. -equivalence
   d. Complement

3. In mathematics, two vectors are _____ if they are perpendicular, i.e., they form a right angle. The word comes from the Greek á½€ρθÏŒς , meaning 'straight', and γωνῖα (gonia), meaning 'angle'. For example, a subway and the street above, although they do not physically intersect, are _____ if they cross at a right angle.
   a. Embedding
   b. Unital
   c. Expression
   d. Orthogonal

4. In the mathematical fields of linear algebra and functional analysis, the _____ $W^\perp$ of a subspace W of an inner product space V is the set of all vectors in V that are orthogonal to every vector in W, i.e., it is

$$W^\perp = \{x \in V : \langle x, y \rangle = 0 \text{ for all } y \in W\}.$$

Informally, it is called the perp, short for perpendicular complement.

The _____ is always closed in the metric topology. In finite-dimensional spaces, that is merely an instance of the fact that all subspaces of a vector space are closed.

a. Euclidean subspace
b. Independent equation
c. Orthogonal complement
d. Invariant subspace

5. A _____ is a concept in geometry. It is a higher-dimensional generalization of the concepts of a line in the plane and a plane in 3-dimensional space. The most familiar kinds of _____ are affine and linear hyperplanes; less familiar is the projective _____.
   a. Cusp
   b. Hyperplane
   c. Kodaira embedding theorem
   d. Polar homology

6. In mathematics, a _____ is a rectangular array of numbers. This way, matrices can record data that depend on multiple parameters. In particular they are used to keep track of the coefficients of multiple linear equations. Matrices are closely connected to linear transformations, which are higher-dimensional analogs of linear functions, i.e., functions of the form f(x) = c Â· x, where c is a constant. This map corresponds to a _____ with one row and column, with entry c. In addition to a number of elementary, entrywise operations such as _____ addition a key notion is _____ multiplication, which displays a number of features not encountered in numbers; for example, products of matrices depend on the order of the factors, unlike products of real numbers, say, where c Â· d = d Â· c for any two numbers c and d.
   a. Heap
   b. Polynomial expression
   c. Commutativity
   d. Matrix

7. Definition. Two vector subspaces A and B of an inner product space V are called _____ if each vector in A is orthogonal to each vector in B. The largest subspace that is orthogonal to a given subspace is its orthogonal complement.
   a. AKS primality test
   b. Abelian P-root group
   c. ADE classification
   d. Orthogonal subspaces

8. In linear algebra, a _____ is a set of vectors that, in a linear combination, can represent every vector in a given vector space or free module, and such that no element of the set can be represented as a linear combination of the others. In other words, a _____ is a linearly independent spanning set.

a. Supergroup
b. Chirality
c. Basis
d. Minor

9. In linear algebra, two vectors in an inner product space are _____ if they are orthogonal and both of unit length. A set of vectors form an _____ set if all vectors in the set are mutually orthogonal and all of unit length. An _____ set which forms a basis is called an _____ basis.

a. Invertible matrix
b. Elementary matrix
c. Overdetermined
d. Orthonormal

10. In mathematics, an _____ of an inner product space V (i.e., a vector space with an inner product), is a set of mutually orthogonal vectors of magnitude 1 (unit vectors) that span the space when infinite linear combinations are allowed. (In some contexts, especially in linear algebra, the concept of basis (linear algebra) means a set of vectors that span a space when only finite linear combinations are allowed.) Such an infinite linear combination is an infinite series, and the concept of convergence relied upon is defined in terms of the space's inner product.

a. Overdetermined
b. Eigendecomposition
c. Orthonormal basis
d. Orientation

11. In linear algebra, an _____ is a square matrix with real entries whose columns (or rows) are orthogonal unit vectors (i.e., orthonormal.) Equivalently, a matrix Q is orthogonal if its transpose is equal to its inverse:

$$Q^T Q = QQ^T = I.$$

As a linear transformation, an _____ preserves the dot product of vectors, and therefore acts as an isometry of Euclidean space, such as a rotation or reflection.

The set of n × n orthogonal matrices forms a group O(n), known as the orthogonal group.

a. Unimodular matrix
b. Unistochastic matrix
c. Alternating sign matrix
d. Orthogonal matrix

12. In mathematics, the _____ of a ring R, often denoted char(R), is defined to be the smallest number of times one must add the ring's multiplicative identity element (1) to itself to get the additive identity element (0); the ring is said to have _____ zero if this repeated sum never reaches the additive identity. That is, char(R) is the smallest positive number n such that

$$\underbrace{1 + \cdots + 1}_{n \text{ summands}} = 0$$

if such a number n exists, and 0 otherwise. The _____ may also be taken to be the exponent of the ring's additive group, that is, the smallest positive n such that

$$\underbrace{a + \cdots + a}_{n \text{ summands}} = 0$$

for every element a of the ring (again, if n exists; otherwise zero.)

a. Characteristic
b. Free ideal ring
c. Coherent ring
d. Hereditary

13. In linear algebra, a square matrix A is called diagonalizable if it is similar to a diagonal matrix, i.e., if there exists an invertible matrix P such that $P^{-1}AP$ is a diagonal matrix. If V is a finite-dimensional vector space, then a linear map $T : V \to V$ is called diagonalizable if there exists a basis of V with respect to which T is represented by a diagonal matrix. Diagonalization is the process of finding a corresponding diagonal matrix for a _____ or linear map.

a. Pascal matrix
b. Hamiltonian matrix
c. Cauchy matrix
d. Diagonalizable matrix

14. In mathematics, for a given complex Hermitian matrix A and nonzero vector x, the _____ R(A,x) is defined as:

$$\frac{x^* A x}{x^* x}.$$

For real matrices and vectors, the condition of being Hermitian reduces to that of being symmetric, and the conjugate transpose x^* to the usual transpose x'. Note that R(A,cx) = R(A,x) for any real scalar c. Recall that a Hermitian (or real symmetric) matrix has real eigenvalues.

a. Reality structure
b. Vectorization
c. Rayleigh quotient
d. Projection-valued measure

15. In linear algebra, a _____ is a linear transformation that squares to the identity ($R^2 = I$, where R is in K dimensional space), also known as an involution in the general linear group. In addition to reflections across hyperplanes, the class of general reflections includes point reflections, reflections across subspaces of intermediate dimension, and non-orthogonal reflections.

A _____ over a hyperplane in an inner product space is necessarily symmetric, but a general _____ need not be as the example $\begin{bmatrix} 1 & 0 \\ 1 & -1 \end{bmatrix}$ shows.

a. Reflection
b. Morphism
c. Homomorphic secret sharing
d. Shear mappings

16. In mathematics, a system of linear equations is considered _____ if there are more equations than unknowns. The terminology can be described in terms of the concept of counting constants. Each unknown can be seen as an available degree of freedom.
a. Elementary matrix
b. Orthogonalization
c. Euclidean subspace
d. Overdetermined

17. In geometry, a _____ is a surface of revolution in the shape of a helix with thickness, generated by revolving a circle about the path of a helix. The torus is a special case of the _____ obtained when the helix is crushed to a circle.

A _____ wrapped around the z-axis can be defined parametrically by:

$$x(u,v) = (R + r\cos v)\cos u,$$
$$y(u,v) = (R + r\cos v)\sin u,$$
$$z(u,v) = r\sin v + \frac{P \cdot u}{\pi},$$

where

$$u \in [0,\ 2n\pi]\ (n \in \mathbb{R}),$$
$$v \in [0,\ 2\pi],$$

R is the distance from the center of the tube to the center of the helix,
r is the radius of the tube,
P is the speed of the movement along the z axis (in a right-handed Cartesian coordinate system, positive values create right-handed springs, whereas negative values create left-handed springs),
n is the number of rounds in circle.

a. Spring
b. Ruled surfaces
c. Steiner surfaces
d. PDE surfaces

18. The most commonly encountered form of Hooke's law is probably the spring equation, which relates the force exerted by a spring to the distance it is stretched by a _____, k, measured in force per length.

$$F = -kx$$

The negative sign indicates that the force exerted by the spring is in direct opposition to the direction of displacement. It is called a 'restoring force', as it tends to restore the system to equilibrium.

a. -equivalence
b. 2-bridge knot
c. -module
d. Spring constant

19. The method of _____ is used to approximately solve overdetermined systems, i.e. systems of equations in which there are more equations than unknowns. _____ is often applied in statistical contexts, particularly regression analysis.

_____ can be interpreted as a method of fitting data.

a. -module
b. 2-bridge knot
c. -equivalence
d. Least squares

Chapter 7. CHANGE OF BASIS

1. In algebraic topology, a simplicial k-_____ is a formal linear combination of k-simplices.

Integration is defined on chains by taking the linear combination of integrals over the simplices in the _____ with coefficients typically integers. The set of all k-chains forms a group and the sequence of these groups is called a _____ complex.

   a. Bockstein homomorphism
   b. Chain
   c. Tesseract
   d. Combinatorial topology

2. In mathematics, the _____ of a ring R, often denoted char(R), is defined to be the smallest number of times one must add the ring's multiplicative identity element (1) to itself to get the additive identity element (0); the ring is said to have _____ zero if this repeated sum never reaches the additive identity. That is, char(R) is the smallest positive number n such that

$$\underbrace{1 + \cdots + 1}_{n \text{ summands}} = 0$$

if such a number n exists, and 0 otherwise. The _____ may also be taken to be the exponent of the ring's additive group, that is, the smallest positive n such that

$$\underbrace{a + \cdots + a}_{n \text{ summands}} = 0$$

for every element a of the ring (again, if n exists; otherwise zero.)

   a. Characteristic
   b. Free ideal ring
   c. Coherent ring
   d. Hereditary

3. In linear algebra, a _____ or column matrix is an m × 1 matrix, i.e. a matrix consisting of a single column of m elements.

Chapter 7. CHANGE OF BASIS

$$\mathbf{x} = \begin{bmatrix} x_1 \\ x_2 \\ \vdots \\ x_m \end{bmatrix}$$

The transpose of a _____ is a row vector and vice versa.

The set of all column vectors forms a vector space which is the dual space to the set of all row vectors.

a. K-frame
b. Column vector
c. Symplectic vector space
d. Normal basis

4. In linear algebra, a _____ is an explicit representation of a vector in an abstract vector space as an ordered list of numbers or, equivalently, as an element of the coordinate space F^n. Coordinate vectors allow calculations with abstract objects to be transformed into calculations with blocks of numbers (matrices and column vectors.)

Let V be a vector space of dimension n over a field F and let

$$B = \{b_1, b_2, \ldots, b_n\}$$

be an ordered basis for V. Then for every $v \in V$ there is a unique linear combination of the basis vectors that equals v:

$$v = \alpha_1 b_1 + \alpha_2 b_2 + \cdots + \alpha_n b_n$$

$$v_B = (\alpha_1, \alpha_2, \cdots, \alpha_n)$$

This is also called the representation of v with respect of B, or the B representation of v.

a. Homogeneous coordinates
b. Coordinate vector
c. Cofactor
d. Direction vector

Chapter 7. CHANGE OF BASIS 75

5. In mathematics, a _____ is a rectangular array of numbers. This way, matrices can record data that depend on multiple parameters. In particular they are used to keep track of the coefficients of multiple linear equations. Matrices are closely connected to linear transformations, which are higher-dimensional analogs of linear functions, i.e., functions of the form f(x) = c Â· x, where c is a constant. This map corresponds to a _____ with one row and column, with entry c. In addition to a number of elementary, entrywise operations such as _____ addition a key notion is _____ multiplication, which displays a number of features not encountered in numbers; for example, products of matrices depend on the order of the factors, unlike products of real numbers, say, where c Â· d = d Â· c for any two numbers c and d.
   a. Polynomial expression
   b. Commutativity
   c. Heap
   d. Matrix

6. In linear algebra, the _____ states that every square matrix over the real or complex field satisfies its own characteristic equation.

More precisely; if A is the given n×n matrix and I_n is the n×n identity matrix, then the characteristic polynomial of A is defined as:

where 'det' is the determinant function. The _____ states that substituting the matrix A in the characteristic polynomial (which involves multiplying its constant term by I_n, since that is the zeroth power of A) results in the zero matrix:

The _____ also holds for square matrices over commutative rings.

   a. 2-bridge knot
   b. Cayley-Hamilton theorem
   c. -equivalence
   d. -module

7. A _____ is a method used by a computer language to store matrices of more than one dimension in memory.

Fortran and C use different schemes. Fortran uses 'Column Major', in which all the elements for a given column are stored contiguously in memory.

Chapter 7. CHANGE OF BASIS

  a. Moment matrix
  b. Polynomial matrix
  c. Skew-Hermitian matrix
  d. Matrix representation

8. In mathematics, for a given complex Hermitian matrix A and nonzero vector x, the _____ R(A,x) is defined as:

$$\frac{x^* A x}{x^* x}.$$

For real matrices and vectors, the condition of being Hermitian reduces to that of being symmetric, and the conjugate transpose x* to the usual transpose x'. Note that R(A,cx) = R(A,x) for any real scalar c. Recall that a Hermitian (or real symmetric) matrix has real eigenvalues.

  a. Rayleigh quotient
  b. Vectorization
  c. Projection-valued measure
  d. Reality structure

9. In linear algebra, two n-by-n matrices A and B are called _____ if

$$B = P^{-1} A P$$

for some invertible n-by-n matrix P. _____ matrices represent the same linear transformation under two different bases, with P being the change of basis matrix.

The matrix P is sometimes called a similarity transformation. In the context of matrix groups, similarity is sometimes referred to as conjugacy, with _____ matrices being conjugate.

  a. Similar
  b. Zero matrix
  c. Cartan matrix
  d. Skew-symmetric

10. One of the meanings of the terms _____ and _____ transformation (also called dilation) of a Euclidean space is a function f from the space into itself that multiplies all distances by the same positive scalar r, so that for any two points x and y we have

$$d(f(x), f(y)) = rd(x,y),$$

where 'd(x,y)' is the Euclidean distance from x to y. Two sets are called similar if one is the image of the other under such a _____.

A special case is a homothetic transformation or central _____: it neither involves rotation nor taking the mirror image.

a. Plane
b. -module
c. -equivalence
d. Similarity

11. In linear algebra, a square matrix A is called diagonalizable if it is similar to a diagonal matrix, i.e., if there exists an invertible matrix P such that $P^{-1}AP$ is a diagonal matrix. If V is a finite-dimensional vector space, then a linear map T : V → V is called diagonalizable if there exists a basis of V with respect to which T is represented by a diagonal matrix. Diagonalization is the process of finding a corresponding diagonal matrix for a _____ or linear map.
a. Hamiltonian matrix
b. Diagonalizable matrix
c. Cauchy matrix
d. Pascal matrix

Chapter 8. EIGENVALUES: FURTHER APPLICATIONS AND COMPUTATIONS

1. In mathematics, the _____ are the following sequence of numbers:

   The first two _____ are 0 and 1, and each remaining number is the sum of the previous two:

   Some sources omit the initial 0, instead beginning the sequence with two 1s.

   In mathematical terms, the sequence F_n of _____ is defined by the recurrence relation

   with seed values

   a. Fibonacci numbers
   b. -equivalence
   c. 2-bridge knot
   d. -module

2. In mathematics, a _____ is a homogeneous polynomial of degree two in a number of variables. For example,

   $$4x^2 + 2xy - 3y^2$$

   is a _____ in the variables x and y.

   Quadratic forms are central objects in mathematics, occurring for instance in number theory, geometry (Riemannian metric), topology (intersection forms on homology), and Lie theory (the Killing form.)

   a. Rank
   b. Homogeneous coordinates
   c. Quadratic form
   d. Partial trace

Chapter 8. EIGENVALUES: FURTHER APPLICATIONS AND COMPUTATIONS

3. In mathematics, a _____ is a constant multiplicative factor of a certain object. For example, in the expression $9x^2$, the _____ of x^2 is 9.

The object can be such things as a variable, a vector, a function, etc.

a. Vandermonde polynomial
b. Coefficient
c. Tschirnhaus transformation
d. Constant term

4. In linear algebra, the _____ refers to a matrix consisting of the coefficients of the variables in a set of linear equations.

In general, a system with m linear equations and n unknowns can be written as

$$a_{11}x_1 + a_{12}x_2 + ... + a_{1n}x_n = b_1$$
$$a_{21}x_1 + a_{22}x_2 + ... + a_{2n}x_n = b_2$$
$$\vdots$$
$$a_{m1}x_1 + a_{m2}x_2 + ... + a_{mn}x_n = b_m$$

where $x_1, x_2, ..., x_n$ are the unknowns and the numbers $a_{11}, a_{12}, ..., a_{mn}$ are the coefficients of the system. The _____ is the mxn matrix with the coefficient a_{ij} as the (i,j)-th entry:

$$\begin{bmatrix} a_{11} & a_{12} & \cdots & a_{1n} \\ a_{21} & a_{22} & \cdots & a_{2n} \\ \vdots & \vdots & \ddots & \vdots \\ a_{m1} & a_{m2} & \cdots & a_{mn} \end{bmatrix}$$

a. Centrosymmetric matrix
b. Linear inequality
c. Segre classification
d. Coefficient matrix

5. In linear algebra, a square matrix A is called diagonalizable if it is similar to a diagonal matrix, i.e., if there exists an invertible matrix P such that $P^{-1}AP$ is a diagonal matrix. If V is a finite-dimensional vector space, then a linear map $T : V \to V$ is called diagonalizable if there exists a basis of V with respect to which T is represented by a diagonal matrix. Diagonalization is the process of finding a corresponding diagonal matrix for a _____ or linear map.

a. Diagonalizable matrix
b. Pascal matrix
c. Cauchy matrix
d. Hamiltonian matrix

6. In mathematics, a _____ is a rectangular array of numbers. This way, matrices can record data that depend on multiple parameters. In particular they are used to keep track of the coefficients of multiple linear equations. Matrices are closely connected to linear transformations, which are higher-dimensional analogs of linear functions, i.e., functions of the form f(x) = c Â· x, where c is a constant. This map corresponds to a _____ with one row and column, with entry c. In addition to a number of elementary, entrywise operations such as _____ addition a key notion is _____ multiplication, which displays a number of features not encountered in numbers; for example, products of matrices depend on the order of the factors, unlike products of real numbers, say, where c Â· d = d Â· c for any two numbers c and d.
a. Heap
b. Commutativity
c. Polynomial expression
d. Matrix

7. In linear algebra, the _____ of a matrix A is another matrix A^T (also written A', A^{tr} or ^tA) created by any one of the following equivalent actions:

- write the rows of A as the columns of A^T
- write the columns of A as the rows of A^T
- reflect A by its main diagonal (which starts from the top left) to obtain A^T

Formally, the _____ of an m × n matrix A with elements A_{ij} is the n × m matrix

$$A^T_{ij} = A_{ji} \text{ for } 1 \leq i \leq n, 1 \leq j \leq m.$$

Chapter 8. EIGENVALUES: FURTHER APPLICATIONS AND COMPUTATIONS

The _____ of a scalar is the same scalar.

- $[1 \ 2]^T = \begin{bmatrix} 1 \\ 2 \end{bmatrix}$.

- $\begin{bmatrix} 1 & 2 \\ 3 & 4 \end{bmatrix}^T = \begin{bmatrix} 1 & 3 \\ 2 & 4 \end{bmatrix}$.

- $\begin{bmatrix} 1 & 2 \\ 3 & 4 \\ 5 & 6 \end{bmatrix}^T = \begin{bmatrix} 1 & 3 & 5 \\ 2 & 4 & 6 \end{bmatrix}$.

For matrices A, B and scalar c we have the following properties of _____:

1. $\left(\mathbf{A}^T\right)^T = \mathbf{A}$

    Taking the _____ is an involution (self inverse.)

- $(\mathbf{A} + \mathbf{B})^T = \mathbf{A}^T + \mathbf{B}^T$

    The _____ respects addition.

- $(\mathbf{AB})^T = \mathbf{B}^T \mathbf{A}^T$

    Note that the order of the factors reverses. From this one can deduce that a square matrix A is invertible if and only if A^T is invertible, and in this case we have $(A^{-1})^T = (A^T)^{-1}$. It is relatively easy to extend this result to the general case of multiple matrices, where we find that $(ABC...XYZ)^T = Z^T Y^T X^T ... C^T B^T A^T$.

- $(c\mathbf{A})^T = c\mathbf{A}^T$

    The _____ of a scalar is the same scalar. Together with (2), this states that the _____ is a linear map from the space of m × n matrices to the space of all n × m matrices.

- $\det(\mathbf{A}^T) = \det(\mathbf{A})$

    The determinant of a square matrix is the same as that of its _____.

- The dot product of two column vectors a and b can be computed as

Chapter 8. EIGENVALUES: FURTHER APPLICATIONS AND COMPUTATIONS

$$\mathbf{a} \cdot \mathbf{b} = \mathbf{a}^T \mathbf{b},$$

which is written as $a_i\, b^i$ in Einstein notation.

- If A has only real entries, then $A^T A$ is a positive-semidefinite matrix.
- $(\mathbf{A}^T)^{-1} = (\mathbf{A}^{-1})^T$

  The _____ of an invertible matrix is also invertible, and its inverse is the _____ of the inverse of the original matrix.

- If A is a square matrix, then its eigenvalues are equal to the eigenvalues of its _____.

A square matrix whose _____ is equal to itself is called a symmetric matrix; that is, A is symmetric if

$$\mathbf{A}^T = \mathbf{A}.$$

A square matrix whose _____ is also its inverse is called an orthogonal matrix; that is, G is orthogonal if

$$\mathbf{G}\mathbf{G}^T = \mathbf{G}^T\mathbf{G} = \mathbf{I}_n,$$ the identity matrix, i.e. $G^T = G^{-1}$.

A square matrix whose _____ is equal to its negative is called skew-symmetric matrix; that is, A is skew-symmetric if

$$\mathbf{A}^T = -\mathbf{A}.$$

The conjugate _____ of the complex matrix A, written as A^*, is obtained by taking the _____ of A and the complex conjugate of each entry:

$$\mathbf{A}^* = (\overline{\mathbf{A}})^T = \overline{(\mathbf{A}^T)}.$$

If f: V→W is a linear map between vector spaces V and W with nondegenerate bilinear forms, we define the _____ of f to be the linear map ${}^t f$: W→V, determined by

$$B_V(v, {}^t f(w)) = B_W(f(v), w) \quad \forall\, v \in V, w \in W.$$

Here, B_V and B_W are the bilinear forms on V and W respectively. The matrix of the _____ of a map is the transposed matrix only if the bases are orthonormal with respect to their bilinear forms.

Over a complex vector space, one often works with sesquilinear forms instead of bilinear (conjugate-linear in one argument.)

Chapter 8. EIGENVALUES: FURTHER APPLICATIONS AND COMPUTATIONS

a. Levinson recursion
b. Drazin inverse
c. Tridiagonal matrix
d. Transpose

8. The set of all symmetry operations considered, on all objects in a set X, can be modeled as a group action g : G × X → X, where the image of g in G and x in X is written as gÂ·x. If, for some g, gÂ·x = y then x and y are said to be symmetrical to each other. For each object x, operations g for which gÂ·x = x form a group, the _____ of the object, a subgroup of G. If the _____ of x is the trivial group then x is said to be asymmetric, otherwise symmetric.

a. 2-bridge knot
b. Symmetry group
c. -equivalence
d. -module

9. In mathematics, the _____ of a number n is the number that, when added to n, yields zero. The _____ of F is denoted −F.

For example, the _____ of 7 is −7, because 7 + (−7) = 0, and the _____ of −0.3 is 0.3, because −0.3 + 0.3 = 0.

a. Isomorphism class
b. Interior algebra
c. Artinian ideal
d. Additive inverse

10. In mathematics, an _____ on a real vector space is a choice of which ordered bases are 'positively' oriented and which are 'negatively' oriented. In the three-dimensional Euclidean space, the two possible basis orientations are called right-handed and left-handed (or right-chiral and left-chiral), respectively. However, the choice of _____ is independent of the handedness or chirality of the bases (although right-handed bases are typically declared to be positively oriented, they may also be assigned a negative _____.)

a. Orientation
b. Orthogonal Procrustes problem
c. Elementary matrix
d. Overdetermined

11. In linear algebra, a _____ or row matrix is a 1 × n matrix, that is, a matrix consisting of a single row:

Chapter 8. EIGENVALUES: FURTHER APPLICATIONS AND COMPUTATIONS

$$\mathbf{x} = \begin{bmatrix} x_1 & x_2 & \ldots & x_m \end{bmatrix}.$$

The transpose of a _____ is a column vector:

$$\begin{bmatrix} x_1 \\ x_2 \\ \vdots \\ x_m \end{bmatrix} = \begin{bmatrix} x_1 & x_2 & \ldots & x_m \end{bmatrix}^T.$$

The set of all row vectors forms a vector space which is the dual space to the set of all column vectors.

Row vectors are sometimes written using the following non-standard notation:

$$\mathbf{x} = \begin{bmatrix} x_1, x_2, \ldots, x_m \end{bmatrix}.$$

- Matrix multiplication involves the action of multiplying each _____ of one matrix by each column vector of another matrix.

- The dot product of two vectors a and b is equivalent to multiplying the _____ representation of a by the column vector representation of b:

$$\mathbf{a} \cdot \mathbf{b} = \begin{bmatrix} a_1 & a_2 & a_3 \end{bmatrix} \begin{bmatrix} b_1 \\ b_2 \\ b_3 \end{bmatrix}.$$

a. Row vector
b. Dual number
c. Polynomial basis
d. Dual spaces

12. In the mathematical fields of geometry and linear algebra, a principal axis is a certain line in a Euclidean space associated to an ellipsoid or hyperboloid, generalizing the major and minor axes of an ellipse. The _____ states that the principal axes are perpendicular, and gives a constructive procedure for finding them.

Mathematically, the _____ is a generalization of the method of completing the square from elementary algebra.

Chapter 8. EIGENVALUES: FURTHER APPLICATIONS AND COMPUTATIONS

  a. Rank
  b. Homogeneous function
  c. Barycentric coordinates
  d. Principal axis theorem

13. In linear algebra, a _____ or column matrix is an m × 1 matrix, i.e. a matrix consisting of a single column of m elements.

$$\mathbf{x} = \begin{bmatrix} x_1 \\ x_2 \\ \vdots \\ x_m \end{bmatrix}$$

The transpose of a _____ is a row vector and vice versa.

The set of all column vectors forms a vector space which is the dual space to the set of all row vectors.

  a. Normal basis
  b. K-frame
  c. Symplectic vector space
  d. Column vector

14. In mathematics, a _____ is a curve obtained by intersecting a cone (more precisely, a circular conical surface) with a plane. A _____ is therefore a restriction of a quadric surface to the plane. The conic sections were named and studied as long ago as 200 BC, when Apollonius of Perga undertook a systematic study of their properties.
  a. Matrix representation of conic sections
  b. Dandelin spheres
  c. Conic section
  d. Derivation of the cartesian form for an ellipse

15. In mathematics, an _____ is the finite or bounded case of a conic section, the geometric shape that results from cutting a circular conical or cylindrical surface with an oblique plane. It is also the locus of all points of the plane whose distances to two fixed points add to the same constant.

Ellipses also arise as images of a circle or a sphere under parallel projection, and some cases of perspective projection.

a. Ellipse
b. AKS primality test
c. ADE classification
d. Abelian P-root group

16. In the mathematical field of topology, a _____ of a fiber bundle, π: E → B, over a topological space, B, is a continuous map, s : B → E, such that π(s(x))=x for all x in B.

A _____ is a certain generalization of the notion of the graph of a function. The graph of a function g : X → Y can be identified with a function taking its values in the Cartesian product E = X×Y of X and Y:

$$s(x) = (x, g(x)) \in E, \quad s : X \to E.$$

A _____ is an abstract characterization of what it means to be a graph.

a. Fiber bundle
b. -equivalence
c. -module
d. Section

17. In mathematics, the _____ is a conic section, the intersection of a right circular conical surface and a plane parallel to a generating straight line of that surface. Given a point (the focus) and a line (the directrix) that lie in a plane, the locus of points in that plane that are equidistant to them is a _____.

A particular case arises when the plane is tangent to the conical surface of a circle.

a. Parabola
b. -module
c. 2-bridge knot
d. -equivalence

18. In mathematics, a _____ is any D-dimensional hypersurface defined as the locus of zeros of a quadratic polynomial. In coordinates $\{x_0, x_1, x_2, \ldots, x_D\}$, the general _____ is defined by the algebraic equation

$$\sum_{i,j=0}^{D} Q_{ij} x_i x_j + \sum_{i=0}^{D} P_i x_i + R = 0$$

Chapter 8. EIGENVALUES: FURTHER APPLICATIONS AND COMPUTATIONS

where Q is a (D + 1)×(D + 1) matrix and P is a (D + 1)-dimensional vector and R a constant. The values Q, P and R are often taken to be real numbers or complex numbers, but in fact, a _____ may be defined over any ring.

a. Noncommutative geometry
b. Relative dimension
c. Quadric
d. Superspace

19. An _____ is a type of quadric surface that is a higher dimensional analogue of an ellipse. The equation of a standard axis-aligned _____ body in an xyz-Cartesian coordinate system is

$$\frac{x^2}{a^2} + \frac{y^2}{b^2} + \frac{z^2}{c^2} = 1$$

where a and b are the equatorial radii (along the x and y axes) and c is the polar radius (along the z-axis), all of which are fixed positive real numbers determining the shape of the _____.

More generally, a not-necessarily-axis-aligned _____ is defined by the equation

$$\mathbf{x}^T A \mathbf{x} = 1$$

where A is a symmetric positive definite matrix and x is a vector.

a. ADE classification
b. Abelian P-root group
c. Ellipsoid
d. AKS primality test

20. In topology, especially algebraic topology, the _____ CX of a topological space X is the quotient space:

$$CX = (X \times I)/(X \times \{0\})$$

of the product of X with the unit interval I = [0, 1]. Intuitively we make X into a cylinder and collapse one end of the cylinder to a point.

If X sits inside Euclidean space, the _____ on X is homeomorphic to the union of lines from X to another point.

a. Cone
b. Descent
c. Smash product
d. Genus

21. The _____ is a doubly ruled surface shaped like a saddle. In a suitable coordinate system, it can be represented by the equation

$$z = \frac{x^2}{a^2} - \frac{y^2}{b^2}.$$

This is a _____ that opens up along the x-axis and down along the y-axis.

Paraboloid of revolution

With a = b an elliptic paraboloid is a paraboloid of revolution: a surface obtained by revolving a parabola around its axis.

a. Hyperbolic paraboloid
b. Prolate spheroid
c. Morin surface
d. Cross-cap

22. In mathematics, a _____ is a quadric, a type of surface in three dimensions, described by the equation

$$\frac{x^2}{a^2} + \frac{y^2}{b^2} - \frac{z^2}{c^2} = 1$$

_____ of one sheet,

or

$$-\frac{x^2}{a^2} - \frac{y^2}{b^2} + \frac{z^2}{c^2} = 1$$

_____ of two sheets.

These are also called elliptical hyperboloids. If, and only if, a = b, it is a _____ of revolution, and is also called a circular _____.

Chapter 8. EIGENVALUES: FURTHER APPLICATIONS AND COMPUTATIONS

a. 2-bridge knot
b. -module
c. -equivalence
d. Hyperboloid

23. In mathematics, a _____ is a quadric surface of special kind. There are two kinds of paraboloids: elliptic and hyperbolic. The elliptic _____ is shaped like an oval cup and can have a maximum or minimum point.
a. Focal surface
b. PDE surfaces
c. Developable surface
d. Paraboloid

24. In linear algebra, the _____ or unit matrix of size n is the n-by-n square matrix with ones on the main diagonal and zeros elsewhere. It is denoted by I_n, or simply by I if the size is immaterial or can be trivially determined by the context. (In some fields, such as quantum mechanics, the _____ is denoted by a boldface one, 1; otherwise it is identical to I.)
a. Identity matrix
b. Orthogonal
c. Associativity
d. Artinian ideal

25. In a totally ordered set all elements are mutually comparable, so such a set can have at most one minimal element and at most one maximal element. Then, due to mutual comparability, the minimal element will also be the least element and the maximal element will also be the greatest element. Thus in a totally ordered set we can simply use the terms _____ and maximum.
a. 2-bridge knot
b. -module
c. -equivalence
d. Minimum

26. is definite, that is, has a real value with the same sign (positive or negative) for all non-zero x. According to that sign, B is called positive definite or _____. If Q takes both positive and negative values, the bilinear form B is called indefinite.
a. 2-bridge knot
b. Negative definite
c. -equivalence
d. -module

Chapter 8. EIGENVALUES: FURTHER APPLICATIONS AND COMPUTATIONS

27. In mathematics, for a given complex Hermitian matrix A and nonzero vector x, the _____ R(A,x) is defined as:

$$\frac{x^* A x}{x^* x}.$$

For real matrices and vectors, the condition of being Hermitian reduces to that of being symmetric, and the conjugate transpose x* to the usual transpose x'. Note that R(A,cx) = R(A,x) for any real scalar c. Recall that a Hermitian (or real symmetric) matrix has real eigenvalues.

a. Vectorization
b. Projection-valued measure
c. Reality structure
d. Rayleigh quotient

28. In mathematics, the _____ is an eigenvalue algorithm: given a matrix A, the algorithm will produce a number λ (the eigenvalue) and a nonzero vector v (the eigenvector), such that Av = λv.

The _____ is a very simple algorithm. It does not compute a matrix decomposition, and hence it can be used when A is a very large sparse matrix.

a. 2-bridge knot
b. -module
c. Power iteration
d. -equivalence

29. In numerical linear algebra, the _____ is an eigenvalue algorithm; that is, a procedure to calculate the eigenvalues and eigenvectors of a matrix. The QR transformation was developed in 1961 by John G.F. Francis (England) and by Vera N. Kublanovskaya (USSR), working independently. The basic idea is to perform a QR decomposition, writing the matrix as a product of an orthogonal matrix and an upper triangular matrix, multiply the factors in the other order, and iterate.

a. QR algorithm
b. -equivalence
c. 2-bridge knot
d. -module

Chapter 9. COMPLEX SCALARS

1. In mathematics, a _____ is any number that can be expressed in the form

$$\frac{a}{b}, a, b \in \mathbb{Z}, b \neq 0$$

which says 'a divided by b, given that a and b are integers and b does not equal zero'. Since the denominator b may be equal to 1, every integer is a _____. The set of all rational numbers is denoted $\mathbb{Q}$ (for quotient.)

   a. Number system
   b. Ratio
   c. Rational number
   d. -equivalence

2. In mathematics, for a given complex Hermitian matrix A and nonzero vector x, the _____ R(A,x) is defined as:

$$\frac{x^* A x}{x^* x}.$$

For real matrices and vectors, the condition of being Hermitian reduces to that of being symmetric, and the conjugate transpose x* to the usual transpose x'. Note that R(A,cx) = R(A,x) for any real scalar c. Recall that a Hermitian (or real symmetric) matrix has real eigenvalues.

   a. Rayleigh quotient
   b. Vectorization
   c. Projection-valued measure
   d. Reality structure

3. In linear algebra, a _____ or column matrix is an m × 1 matrix, i.e. a matrix consisting of a single column of m elements.

$$\mathbf{x} = \begin{bmatrix} x_1 \\ x_2 \\ \vdots \\ x_m \end{bmatrix}$$

The transpose of a _____ is a row vector and vice versa.

The set of all column vectors forms a vector space which is the dual space to the set of all row vectors.

a. Normal basis
b. K-frame
c. Symplectic vector space
d. Column vector

4. In mathematics, the complex numbers are an extension of the real numbers obtained by adjoining an imaginary unit, denoted i, which satisfies:

$$i^2 = -1.$$

Every _____ can be written in the form a + bi, where a and b are real numbers called the real part and the imaginary part of the _____, respectively.

Complex numbers are a field, and thus have addition, subtraction, multiplication, and division operations. These operations extend the corresponding operations on real numbers, although with a number of additional elegant and useful properties, e.g., negative real numbers can be obtained by squaring complex (imaginary) numbers.

a. -module
b. Complex number
c. -equivalence
d. 2-bridge knot

5. In linear algebra, the _____ or unit matrix of size n is the n-by-n square matrix with ones on the main diagonal and zeros elsewhere. It is denoted by I_n, or simply by I if the size is immaterial or can be trivially determined by the context. (In some fields, such as quantum mechanics, the _____ is denoted by a boldface one, 1; otherwise it is identical to I.)
a. Associativity
b. Orthogonal
c. Artinian ideal
d. Identity matrix

6. In mathematics, an _____ is a complex number whose squared value is a real number less than or equal to zero. The imaginary unit, denoted by i or j, is an example of an _____. If y is a real number, then i·y is an _____, because:

$$(i \cdot y)^2 = i^2 \cdot y^2 = -y^2 \leq 0.$$

Imaginary numbers were defined in 1572 by Rafael Bombelli.

Chapter 9. COMPLEX SCALARS

a. ADE classification
b. Abelian P-root group
c. Imaginary number
d. AKS primality test

7. In mathematics, a _____ is a rectangular array of numbers. This way, matrices can record data that depend on multiple parameters. In particular they are used to keep track of the coefficients of multiple linear equations. Matrices are closely connected to linear transformations, which are higher-dimensional analogs of linear functions, i.e., functions of the form f(x) = c Â· x, where c is a constant. This map corresponds to a _____ with one row and column, with entry c. In addition to a number of elementary, entrywise operations such as _____ addition a key notion is _____ multiplication, which displays a number of features not encountered in numbers; for example, products of matrices depend on the order of the factors, unlike products of real numbers, say, where c Â· d = d Â· c for any two numbers c and d.
   a. Matrix
   b. Commutativity
   c. Polynomial expression
   d. Heap

8. In mathematics, in the field of algebraic number theory, a _____ is a formal product of places of an algebraic number field. It is used to encode ramification data for abelian extensions of number field.

   Let K be an algebraic number field with ring of integers R. A _____ is a formal product

   $$m = \prod_p p^{\nu(p)}$$

   where p runs over all places of K, finite or infinite, the exponents v are zero except for finitely many p, for real places r we have v (r)=0 or 1 and for complex places v=0.

   a. Different ideal
   b. Modulus
   c. Principal ideal theorem
   d. Quadratic field

9. In mathematics, the (formal) _____ of a complex vector space V is the complex vector space $\overline{V}$ consisting of all formal complex conjugates of elements of V. That is, $\overline{V}$ is a vector space whose elements are in one-to-one correspondence with the elements of V:

$$\overline{V} = \{\overline{v} \mid v \in V\},$$

with the following rules for addition and scalar multiplication:

$$\overline{v} + \overline{w} = \overline{v+w} \quad \text{and} \quad \alpha\overline{v} = \overline{\overline{\alpha}v}.$$

Here v and w are vectors in V, α is a complex number, and $\overline{\alpha}$ denotes the _____ of α.

In the case where V is a linear subspace of $\mathbb{C}^n$, the formal _____ $\overline{V}$ is naturally isomorphic to the actual _____ subspace of V in $\mathbb{C}^n$.

a. Conjugate transpose
b. Complex conjugate
c. Binomial inverse theorem
d. Polynomial basis

10. In algebra, a _____ of an element in a quadratic extension field of a field K is its image under the unique non-identity automorphism of the extended field that fixes K. If the extension is generated by a square root of an element r of K, then the _____ of $a + b\sqrt{r}$ is $a - b\sqrt{r}$ for $a, b \in K$, and in particular in the case of the field C of complex numbers as an extension of the field R of real numbers (where r = − 1), the complex _____ of a + bi is a − bi.

Forming the sum or product of any element of the extension field with its _____ always gives an element of K. This can be used to rewrite a quotient of numbers in the extended field so that the denominator lies in K, by multiplying numerator and denominator by the _____ of the denominator. This process is called rationalization of the denominator, in particular if K is the field Q of rational numbers.

a. Conjugate
b. K-theory
c. Digital root
d. Field arithmetic

11. In mathematics, the _____ are the following sequence of numbers:

>

Chapter 9. COMPLEX SCALARS

The first two _____ are 0 and 1, and each remaining number is the sum of the previous two:

Some sources omit the initial 0, instead beginning the sequence with two 1s.

In mathematical terms, the sequence F_n of _____ is defined by the recurrence relation

with seed values

a. -module
b. -equivalence
c. 2-bridge knot
d. Fibonacci numbers

12. In abstract algebra, a _____ is an algebraic structure with notions of addition, subtraction, multiplication and division, satisfying certain axioms. The most commonly used fields are the _____ of real numbers, the _____ of complex numbers, and the _____ of rational numbers, but there are also finite fields, fields of functions, various algebraic number fields, p-adic fields, and so forth.

Any _____ may be used as the scalars for a vector space, which is the standard general context for linear algebra.

a. Tensor product of fields
b. Generic polynomial
c. Separable
d. Field

13. In mathematics, a _____ of a number x is any number which, when repeatedly multiplied by itself, eventually yields x:

$$r \times r \times \cdots \times r = x.$$

In terms of exponentiation, r is a _____ of x if

$$r^n = x$$

for some positive integer n. For example, 2 is a _____ of 16 since $2^4 = 2 \times 2 \times 2 \times 2 = 16$.

The number n is called the degree of the _____.

a. Difference of two squares
b. Cubic function
c. Rationalisation
d. Root

14. An nth _____, where n = 1,2,3,···, is a complex number, z, satisfying the equation

$$z^n = 1.$$

Second roots are called square roots, and third roots are called cube roots.

An nth _____ is primitive if

$$z^k \neq 1 \qquad (k = 1, 2, 3, \ldots, n-1).$$

There are n different nth roots of unity:

$$z^k \qquad (k = 1, 2, 3, \ldots, n),$$

where z is any primitive nth _____. These n roots are distributed evenly over the unit circle as can be seen in the plot on the right-hand side of the three 3rd roots of unity.

a. 2-bridge knot
b. -equivalence
c. -module
d. Root of unity

15. _____ is the mathematical process of putting things together. The plus sign '+' means that numbers are added together. For example, in the picture on the right, there are 3 + 2 apples--meaning three apples and two other apples--which is the same as five apples, since 3 + 2 = 5.

a. Abelian P-root group
b. ADE classification
c. AKS primality test
d. Addition

16. In mathematics, the _____ of a ring R, often denoted char(R), is defined to be the smallest number of times one must add the ring's multiplicative identity element (1) to itself to get the additive identity element (0); the ring is said to have _____ zero if this repeated sum never reaches the additive identity. That is, char(R) is the smallest positive number n such that

$$\underbrace{1 + \cdots + 1}_{n \text{ summands}} = 0$$

if such a number n exists, and 0 otherwise. The _____ may also be taken to be the exponent of the ring's additive group, that is, the smallest positive n such that

$$\underbrace{a + \cdots + a}_{n \text{ summands}} = 0$$

for every element a of the ring (again, if n exists; otherwise zero.)

a. Hereditary
b. Coherent ring
c. Characteristic
d. Free ideal ring

17. In linear algebra, functional analysis and related areas of mathematics, a _____ is a function that assigns a strictly positive length or size to all vectors in a vector space, other than the zero vector. A seminorm (or pseudonorm), on the other hand, is allowed to assign zero length to some non-zero vectors.

A simple example is the 2-dimensional Euclidean space R^2 equipped with the Euclidean _____.

a. -module
b. Quasinorm
c. -equivalence
d. Norm

Chapter 9. COMPLEX SCALARS

18. In mathematics, two vectors are _____ if they are perpendicular, i.e., they form a right angle. The word comes from the Greek á½€ρθÏŒς , meaning 'straight', and γωνῖα (gonia), meaning 'angle'. For example, a subway and the street above, although they do not physically intersect, are _____ if they cross at a right angle.
   a. Embedding
   b. Expression
   c. Unital
   d. Orthogonal

19. In mathematics, a _____ in a (unital) ring R is an invertible element of R, i.e. an element u such that there is a v in R with

   uv = vu = 1_R, where 1_R is the multiplicative identity element.

   That is, u is an invertible element of the multiplicative monoid of R. If $0 \neq 1$ in the ring, then 0 is not a _____.

   Unfortunately, the term _____ is also used to refer to the identity element 1_R of the ring, in expressions like ring with a _____ or _____ ring, and also e.g. '_____' matrix.

   a. Ore condition
   b. Ore extension
   c. Unit
   d. Ascending chain condition on principal ideals

20. In mathematics, the _____, Hermitian transpose, or adjoint matrix of an m-by-n matrix A with complex entries is the n-by-m matrix A^* obtained from A by taking the transpose and then taking the complex conjugate of each entry. The _____ is formally defined by

$$(A^*)_{ij} = \overline{A_{ji}}$$

   where the subscripts denote the i,j-th entry, for $1 \leq i \leq n$ and $1 \leq j \leq m$, and the overbar denotes a scalar complex conjugate. (The complex conjugate of a + bi, where a and b are reals, is a − bi.)

   a. Complex conjugate
   b. Change of basis
   c. Dual spaces
   d. Conjugate transpose

Chapter 9. COMPLEX SCALARS

21. In linear algebra, the _____ of a matrix A is another matrix A^T (also written A', A^{tr} or ^tA) created by any one of the following equivalent actions:

- write the rows of A as the columns of A^T
- write the columns of A as the rows of A^T
- reflect A by its main diagonal (which starts from the top left) to obtain A^T

Formally, the _____ of an m × n matrix A with elements A_{ij} is the n × m matrix

$$A^T_{ij} = A_{ji} \text{ for } 1 \leq i \leq n, 1 \leq j \leq m.$$

The _____ of a scalar is the same scalar.

- $$\begin{bmatrix} 1 & 2 \end{bmatrix}^T = \begin{bmatrix} 1 \\ 2 \end{bmatrix}.$$

- $$\begin{bmatrix} 1 & 2 \\ 3 & 4 \end{bmatrix}^T = \begin{bmatrix} 1 & 3 \\ 2 & 4 \end{bmatrix}.$$

- $$\begin{bmatrix} 1 & 2 \\ 3 & 4 \\ 5 & 6 \end{bmatrix}^T = \begin{bmatrix} 1 & 3 & 5 \\ 2 & 4 & 6 \end{bmatrix}.$$

For matrices A, B and scalar c we have the following properties of _____:

1. $$\left(A^T\right)^T = A$$

    Taking the _____ is an involution (self inverse.)

- $$(A + B)^T = A^T + B^T$$

    The _____ respects addition.

- $$(AB)^T = B^T A^T$$

Note that the order of the factors reverses. From this one can deduce that a square matrix A is invertible if and only if A^T is invertible, and in this case we have $(A^{-1})^T = (A^T)^{-1}$. It is relatively easy to extend this result to the general case of multiple matrices, where we find that $(ABC...XYZ)^T = Z^T Y^T X^T...C^T B^T A^T$.

- $(c\mathbf{A})^T = c\mathbf{A}^T$

    The _____ of a scalar is the same scalar. Together with (2), this states that the _____ is a linear map from the space of m × n matrices to the space of all n × m matrices.

- $\det(\mathbf{A}^T) = \det(\mathbf{A})$

    The determinant of a square matrix is the same as that of its _____.

- The dot product of two column vectors a and b can be computed as

    $$\mathbf{a} \cdot \mathbf{b} = \mathbf{a}^T \mathbf{b},$$

which is written as $a_i \, b^i$ in Einstein notation.
- If A has only real entries, then $A^T A$ is a positive-semidefinite matrix.
- $(\mathbf{A}^T)^{-1} = (\mathbf{A}^{-1})^T$

    The _____ of an invertible matrix is also invertible, and its inverse is the _____ of the inverse of the original matrix.

- If A is a square matrix, then its eigenvalues are equal to the eigenvalues of its _____.

A square matrix whose _____ is equal to itself is called a symmetric matrix; that is, A is symmetric if

$$\mathbf{A}^T = \mathbf{A}.$$

A square matrix whose _____ is also its inverse is called an orthogonal matrix; that is, G is orthogonal if

$$\mathbf{G}\mathbf{G}^T = \mathbf{G}^T\mathbf{G} = \mathbf{I}_n,$$ the identity matrix, i.e. $G^T = G^{-1}$.

A square matrix whose _____ is equal to its negative is called skew-symmetric matrix; that is, A is skew-symmetric if

$$\mathbf{A}^T = -\mathbf{A}.$$

The conjugate _____ of the complex matrix A, written as A*, is obtained by taking the _____ of A and the complex conjugate of each entry:

$$\mathbf{A}^* = (\overline{\mathbf{A}})^{\mathrm{T}} = \overline{(\mathbf{A}^{\mathrm{T}})}.$$

If f: V→W is a linear map between vector spaces V and W with nondegenerate bilinear forms, we define the _____ of f to be the linear map $^t f$: W→V, determined by

$$B_V(v, {}^t f(w)) = B_W(f(v), w) \quad \forall\, v \in V, w \in W.$$

Here, B_V and B_W are the bilinear forms on V and W respectively. The matrix of the _____ of a map is the transposed matrix only if the bases are orthonormal with respect to their bilinear forms.

Over a complex vector space, one often works with sesquilinear forms instead of bilinear (conjugate-linear in one argument.)

a. Transpose
b. Tridiagonal matrix
c. Levinson recursion
d. Drazin inverse

22. In mathematics, a _____ is an idealisation of the concept of a matrix, with a focus on the algebraic properties of matrix multiplication. The topic is comparatively obscure within linear algebra, because it entirely ignores the numeric properties of matrices; it is mostly encountered in the context of abstract algebra, especially the theory of semigroups.

Despite the name, matrix units are not the same as unit matrices or unitary matrices.

a. Lie product formula
b. Matrix unit
c. Logarithm of a matrix
d. Laplace expansion

23. In mathematics, a _____ is an n by n complex matrix U satisfying the condition

$$U^*U = UU^* = I_n$$

where I_n is the identity matrix and U^* is the conjugate transpose (also called the Hermitian adjoint) of U. Note this condition says that a matrix U is unitary if and only if it has an inverse which is equal to its conjugate transpose U^*

$$U^{-1} = U^*$$

A _____ in which all entries are real is the same thing as an orthogonal matrix. Just as an orthogonal matrix G preserves the (real) inner product of two real vectors,

$$\langle Gx, Gy \rangle = \langle x, y \rangle$$

so also a _____ U satisfies

$$\langle Ux, Uy \rangle = \langle x, y \rangle$$

for all complex vectors x and y, where $\langle \cdot, \cdot \rangle$ stands now for the standard inner product on C^n. If U is an n by n matrix then the following are all equivalent conditions:

1. U is unitary
2. U^* is unitary
3. the columns of U form an orthonormal basis of C^n with respect to this inner product
4. the rows of U form an orthonormal basis of C^n with respect to this inner product
5. U is an isometry with respect to the norm from this inner product

It follows from the isometry property that all eigenvalues of a _____ are complex numbers of absolute value 1 (i.e., they lie on the unit circle centered at 0 in the complex plane.) The same is true for the determinant.

a. Unimodular matrix
b. Unitary matrix
c. Integer matrix
d. Unistochastic matrix

24. A _____ is a square matrix with complex entries which is equal to its own conjugate transpose -- that is, the element in the ith row and jth column is equal to the complex conjugate of the element in the jth row and ith column, for all indices i and j:

$$a_{i,j} = \overline{a_{j,i}}.$$

Chapter 9. COMPLEX SCALARS

If the conjugate transpose of a matrix A is denoted by $A^\dagger$, then the Hermitian property can be written concisely as

$$A = A^\dagger.$$

For example,

$$\begin{bmatrix} 3 & 2+i \\ 2-i & 1 \end{bmatrix}$$

is a _____.

The entries on the main diagonal (top left to bottom right) of any _____ are necessarily real. A matrix that has only real entries is Hermitian if and only if it is a symmetric matrix, i.e., if it is symmetric with respect to the main diagonal.

a. Hermitian matrix
b. Levinson recursion
c. Permutation matrix
d. Symplectic matrix

25. In linear algebra, a square matrix A is called diagonalizable if it is similar to a diagonal matrix, i.e., if there exists an invertible matrix P such that $P^{-1}AP$ is a diagonal matrix. If V is a finite-dimensional vector space, then a linear map T : V → V is called diagonalizable if there exists a basis of V with respect to which T is represented by a diagonal matrix. Diagonalization is the process of finding a corresponding diagonal matrix for a _____ or linear map.

a. Hamiltonian matrix
b. Cauchy matrix
c. Pascal matrix
d. Diagonalizable matrix

26. For each eigenvector of a linear transformation, there is a corresponding scalar value called an _____ for that vector, which determines the amount the eigenvector is scaled under the linear transformation. For example, an _____ of +2 means that the eigenvector is doubled in length and points in the same direction. An _____ of +1 means that the eigenvector is unchanged, while an _____ of −1 means that the eigenvector is reversed in sense.

Chapter 9. COMPLEX SCALARS

a. ADE classification
b. Abelian P-root group
c. AKS primality test
d. Eigenvalue

27. For each _____ of a linear transformation, there is a corresponding scalar value called an eigenvalue for that vector, which determines the amount the _____ is scaled under the linear transformation. For example, an eigenvalue of +2 means that the _____ is doubled in length and points in the same direction. An eigenvalue of +1 means that the _____ is unchanged, while an eigenvalue of −1 means that the _____ is reversed in sense.

a. AKS primality test
b. ADE classification
c. Abelian P-root group
d. Eigenvector

28. In linear algebra, two n-by-n matrices A and B are called _____ if

$$B = P^{-1}AP$$

for some invertible n-by-n matrix P. _____ matrices represent the same linear transformation under two different bases, with P being the change of basis matrix.

The matrix P is sometimes called a similarity transformation. In the context of matrix groups, similarity is sometimes referred to as conjugacy, with _____ matrices being conjugate.

a. Similar
b. Skew-symmetric
c. Zero matrix
d. Cartan matrix

29. In mathematics, particularly linear algebra and functional analysis, the _____ is any of a number of results about linear operators or about matrices. In broad terms the _____ provides conditions under which an operator or a matrix can be diagonalized (that is, represented as a diagonal matrix in some basis.) This concept of diagonalization is relatively straightforward for operators on finite-dimensional spaces, but requires some modification for operators on infinite-dimensional spaces.

a. Spectral geometry
b. Spectral radius
c. Spectral asymmetry
d. Spectral theorem

Chapter 9. COMPLEX SCALARS

30. A complex square matrix A is a _____ if

    A*A=AA*

where A* is the conjugate transpose of A. That is, a matrix is normal if it commutes with its conjugate transpose.

If A is a real matrix, then $A^*=A^T$; it is normal if $A^TA = AA^T$.

Normality is a convenient test for diagonalizability: every _____ can be converted to a diagonal matrix by a unitary transform, and every matrix which can be made diagonal by a unitary transform is also normal, but finding the desired transform requires much more work than simply testing to see whether the matrix is normal.

a. Duplication matrix
b. Hamiltonian matrix
c. Main diagonal
d. Normal matrix

31. In mathematics and group theory, a _____ system for the action of a group G on a set X is a partition of X that is G-invariant. In terms of the associated equivalence relation on X, G-invariance means that

    x ≡ y implies gx ≡ gy

for all g in G and all x, y in X. The action of G on X determines a natural action of G on any _____ system for X.

Each element of the _____ system is called a _____.

a. Frobenius group
b. Symmetric group
c. Parker vector
d. Block

32. Generally, in mathematics, a _____ of an object is a standard way of presenting that object.

    _____ can also mean a differential form that is defined in a natural (canonical) way; see below.

Suppose we have some set S of objects, with an equivalence relation.

a. Monomial basis
b. Brahmagupta's identity
c. Cylindrical algebraic decomposition
d. Canonical form

33. In linear algebra, a _____ is a set of vectors that, in a linear combination, can represent every vector in a given vector space or free module, and such that no element of the set can be represented as a linear combination of the others. In other words, a _____ is a linearly independent spanning set.
   a. Basis
   b. Chirality
   c. Supergroup
   d. Minor

34. In mathematics, an _____ of a linear mapping

$$T : V \to V$$

from some vector space V to itself is a subspace W of V such that T(W) is contained in W. An _____ of T is also said to be T invariant.

If W is T-invariant, we can restrict T to W to arrive at a new linear mapping

$$T|W : W \to W.$$

Next we give a few immediate examples of invariant subspaces.

   a. Indeterminate system
   b. Invariant subspace
   c. Orthogonal complement
   d. Orthogonal Procrustes problem

Chapter 10. SOLVING LARGE LINEAR SYSTEMS

1. In algebraic geometry, a _____ is a special sort of birational map between varieties. The first example, known as the Atiyah _____, was found in .
   a. Blowing up
   b. -equivalence
   c. Cremona group
   d. Flop

2. In group theory, a branch of mathematics, the term _____ is used in two closely related senses:

   - the _____ of a group is its cardinality, i.e. the number of its elements;
   - the _____, sometimes period, of an element a of a group is the smallest positive integer m such that $a^m = e$ (where e denotes the identity element of the group, and a^m denotes the product of m copies of a.) If no such m exists, we say that a has infinite _____. All elements of finite groups have finite _____.

   We denote the _____ of a group G by ord(G) or $|G|$ and the _____ of an element a by ord(a) or $|a|$.

   Example. The symmetric group S_3 has the following multiplication table.

   This group has six elements, so ord(S_3) = 6.

   a. Outer automorphism group
   b. Index calculus algorithm
   c. Artin group
   d. Order

3. In mathematics, a _____ is a semigroup in which every element is idempotent The lattice of varieties of bands was described independently by Birjukov, Fennemore and Gerhard. Semilattices, left-zero bands, right-zero bands, rectangular bands and regular bands, specific subclasses of bands which lie near the bottom of this lattice, are of particular interest and are briefly described below.
   a. Formal power series
   b. Band
   c. Group extension
   d. Direct product

4. In mathematics, particularly matrix theory, a _____ is a sparse matrix, whose non-zero entries are confined to a diagonal band, comprising the main diagonal and zero or more diagonals on either side.

Formally, an n×n matrix A=(a_{i,j}) is a _____ if all matrix elements are zero outside a diagonally bordered band whose range is determined by constants k_1 and k_2:

$$a_{i,j} = 0 \quad \text{if} \quad j < i - k_1 \quad \text{or} \quad j > i + k_2; \quad k_1, k_2 \geq 0.$$

The quantities k_1 and k_2 are the left and right half-bandwidth, respectively. The bandwidth of the matrix is $k_1 + k_2 + 1$ (in other words, the smallest number of adjacent diagonals to which the non-zero elements are confined.)

a. Skew-symmetric
b. Modal matrix
c. Binary matrix
d. Band matrix

5. In algebraic topology, a simplicial k-_____ is a formal linear combination of k-simplices.

Integration is defined on chains by taking the linear combination of integrals over the simplices in the _____ with coefficients typically integers. The set of all k-chains forms a group and the sequence of these groups is called a _____ complex.

a. Tesseract
b. Combinatorial topology
c. Bockstein homomorphism
d. Chain

6. In mathematics, a _____ is a rectangular array of numbers. This way, matrices can record data that depend on multiple parameters. In particular they are used to keep track of the coefficients of multiple linear equations. Matrices are closely connected to linear transformations, which are higher-dimensional analogs of linear functions, i.e., functions of the form f(x) = c Â· x, where c is a constant. This map corresponds to a _____ with one row and column, with entry c. In addition to a number of elementary, entrywise operations such as _____ addition a key notion is _____ multiplication, which displays a number of features not encountered in numbers; for example, products of matrices depend on the order of the factors, unlike products of real numbers, say, where c Â· d = d Â· c for any two numbers c and d.

a. Polynomial expression
b. Commutativity
c. Heap
d. Matrix

Chapter 10. SOLVING LARGE LINEAR SYSTEMS

7. In linear algebra, the _____ of a matrix A is another matrix A^T (also written A', A^{tr} or ^tA) created by any one of the following equivalent actions:

- write the rows of A as the columns of A^T
- write the columns of A as the rows of A^T
- reflect A by its main diagonal (which starts from the top left) to obtain A^T

Formally, the _____ of an m × n matrix A with elements A_{ij} is the n × m matrix

$$A^T_{ij} = A_{ji} \text{ for } 1 \leq i \leq n, 1 \leq j \leq m.$$

The _____ of a scalar is the same scalar.

- $\begin{bmatrix} 1 & 2 \end{bmatrix}^T = \begin{bmatrix} 1 \\ 2 \end{bmatrix}.$

- $\begin{bmatrix} 1 & 2 \\ 3 & 4 \end{bmatrix}^T = \begin{bmatrix} 1 & 3 \\ 2 & 4 \end{bmatrix}.$

- $\begin{bmatrix} 1 & 2 \\ 3 & 4 \\ 5 & 6 \end{bmatrix}^T = \begin{bmatrix} 1 & 3 & 5 \\ 2 & 4 & 6 \end{bmatrix}.$

For matrices A, B and scalar c we have the following properties of _____:

1. $\left(A^T\right)^T = A$

    Taking the _____ is an involution (self inverse.)

- $(A + B)^T = A^T + B^T$

    The _____ respects addition.

- $(AB)^T = B^T A^T$

Note that the order of the factors reverses. From this one can deduce that a square matrix A is invertible if and only if A^T is invertible, and in this case we have $(A^{-1})^T = (A^T)^{-1}$. It is relatively easy to extend this result to the general case of multiple matrices, where we find that $(ABC...XYZ)^T = Z^TY^TX^T...C^TB^TA^T$.

- $(c\mathbf{A})^T = c\mathbf{A}^T$

   The _____ of a scalar is the same scalar. Together with (2), this states that the _____ is a linear map from the space of m × n matrices to the space of all n × m matrices.

- $\det(\mathbf{A}^T) = \det(\mathbf{A})$

   The determinant of a square matrix is the same as that of its _____.

- The dot product of two column vectors a and b can be computed as

$$\mathbf{a} \cdot \mathbf{b} = \mathbf{a}^T \mathbf{b},$$

which is written as $a_i\, b^i$ in Einstein notation.
- If A has only real entries, then A^TA is a positive-semidefinite matrix.
- $(\mathbf{A}^T)^{-1} = (\mathbf{A}^{-1})^T$

   The _____ of an invertible matrix is also invertible, and its inverse is the _____ of the inverse of the original matrix.

- If A is a square matrix, then its eigenvalues are equal to the eigenvalues of its _____.

A square matrix whose _____ is equal to itself is called a symmetric matrix; that is, A is symmetric if

$$\mathbf{A}^T = \mathbf{A}.$$

A square matrix whose _____ is also its inverse is called an orthogonal matrix; that is, G is orthogonal if

$$\mathbf{G}\mathbf{G}^T = \mathbf{G}^T\mathbf{G} = \mathbf{I}_n,$$ the identity matrix, i.e. $G^T = G^{-1}$.

A square matrix whose _____ is equal to its negative is called skew-symmetric matrix; that is, A is skew-symmetric if

$$\mathbf{A}^T = -\mathbf{A}.$$

The conjugate _____ of the complex matrix A, written as A*, is obtained by taking the _____ of A and the complex conjugate of each entry:

$$\mathbf{A}^* = (\overline{\mathbf{A}})^T = \overline{(\mathbf{A}^T)}.$$

If f: V→W is a linear map between vector spaces V and W with nondegenerate bilinear forms, we define the _____ of f to be the linear map $^t f$: W→V, determined by

$$B_V(v,{}^t f(w)) = B_W(f(v), w) \quad \forall\, v \in V, w \in W.$$

Here, B_V and B_W are the bilinear forms on V and W respectively. The matrix of the _____ of a map is the transposed matrix only if the bases are orthonormal with respect to their bilinear forms.

Over a complex vector space, one often works with sesquilinear forms instead of bilinear (conjugate-linear in one argument.)

a. Tridiagonal matrix
b. Drazin inverse
c. Levinson recursion
d. Transpose

8. In linear algebra, a _____ matrix is a matrix that is 'almost' a diagonal matrix. To be exact: a _____ matrix has nonzero elements only in the main diagonal, the first diagonal below this, and the first diagonal above the main diagonal.

For example, the following matrix is _____:

$$\begin{pmatrix} 1 & 4 & 0 & 0 \\ 3 & 4 & 1 & 0 \\ 0 & 2 & 3 & 4 \\ 0 & 0 & 1 & 3 \end{pmatrix}.$$

A determinant formed from a _____ matrix is known as a continuant.

a. 2-bridge knot
b. Tridiagonal
c. -equivalence
d. -module

9. In linear algebra, a _____ is a matrix that is 'almost' a diagonal matrix. To be exact: a _____ has nonzero elements only in the main diagonal, the first diagonal below this, and the first diagonal above the main diagonal.

For example, the following matrix is tridiagonal:

$$\begin{pmatrix} 1 & 4 & 0 & 0 \\ 3 & 4 & 1 & 0 \\ 0 & 2 & 3 & 4 \\ 0 & 0 & 1 & 3 \end{pmatrix}.$$

A determinant formed from a _____ is known as a continuant.

a. Wilkinson matrices
b. Diagonalizable matrix
c. Similar
d. Tridiagonal matrix

10. In the case of Gaussian elimination, it is best to choose a pivot element with large absolute value. This improves the numerical stability. In _____, the algorithm considers all entries in the column of the matrix that is currently being considered, picks the entry with largest absolute value, and finally swaps rows such that this entry is the pivot in question.
a. -module
b. -equivalence
c. Partial pivoting
d. 2-bridge knot

11. In linear algebra, a _____ or row matrix is a 1 × n matrix, that is, a matrix consisting of a single row:

$$\mathbf{x} = \begin{bmatrix} x_1 & x_2 & \ldots & x_m \end{bmatrix}.$$

The transpose of a _____ is a column vector:

$$\begin{bmatrix} x_1 \\ x_2 \\ \vdots \\ x_m \end{bmatrix} = \begin{bmatrix} x_1 & x_2 & \ldots & x_m \end{bmatrix}^\mathrm{T}.$$

The set of all row vectors forms a vector space which is the dual space to the set of all column vectors.

Row vectors are sometimes written using the following non-standard notation:

$$\mathbf{x} = \begin{bmatrix} x_1, x_2, \ldots, x_m \end{bmatrix}.$$

- Matrix multiplication involves the action of multiplying each _____ of one matrix by each column vector of another matrix.

- The dot product of two vectors a and b is equivalent to multiplying the _____ representation of a by the column vector representation of b:

$$\mathbf{a} \cdot \mathbf{b} = \begin{bmatrix} a_1 & a_2 & a_3 \end{bmatrix} \begin{bmatrix} b_1 \\ b_2 \\ b_3 \end{bmatrix}.$$

a. Polynomial basis
b. Dual number
c. Dual spaces
d. Row vector

12. In linear algebra, a _____ is a square matrix with entries being the unit fractions

$$H_{ij} = \frac{1}{i+j-1}.$$

For example, this is the 5 × 5 _____:

$$H = \begin{bmatrix} 1 & \frac{1}{2} & \frac{1}{3} & \frac{1}{4} & \frac{1}{5} \\ \frac{1}{2} & \frac{1}{3} & \frac{1}{4} & \frac{1}{5} & \frac{1}{6} \\ \frac{1}{3} & \frac{1}{4} & \frac{1}{5} & \frac{1}{6} & \frac{1}{7} \\ \frac{1}{4} & \frac{1}{5} & \frac{1}{6} & \frac{1}{7} & \frac{1}{8} \\ \frac{1}{5} & \frac{1}{6} & \frac{1}{7} & \frac{1}{8} & \frac{1}{9} \end{bmatrix}.$$

The _____ can be regarded as derived from the integral

$$H_{ij} = \int_0^1 x^{i+j-2}\, dx,$$

that is, as a Gramian matrix for powers of x. It arises in the least squares approximation of arbitrary functions by polynomials.

The Hilbert matrices are canonical examples of ill-conditioned matrices, making them notoriously difficult to use in numerical computation.

a. Triangular matrix
b. Hilbert matrix
c. Diagonally dominant
d. Minimum degree algorithm

13. In linear algebra, the _____ or unit matrix of size n is the n-by-n square matrix with ones on the main diagonal and zeros elsewhere. It is denoted by I_n, or simply by I if the size is immaterial or can be trivially determined by the context. (In some fields, such as quantum mechanics, the _____ is denoted by a boldface one, 1; otherwise it is identical to I.)

a. Orthogonal
b. Associativity
c. Artinian ideal
d. Identity matrix

14. In mathematics, a _____ is a collection of linear equations involving the same set of variables. For example,

$$\begin{aligned} 3x + 2y - z &= 1 \\ 2x - 2y + 4z &= -2 \\ -x + \tfrac{1}{2}y - z &= 0 \end{aligned}$$

is a system of three equations in the three variables x, y, z. A solution to a linear system is an assignment of numbers to the variables such that all the equations are simultaneously satisfied.

a. -equivalence
b. -module
c. Simultaneous equations
d. System of linear equations

Chapter 1

1. d	2. a	3. d	4. d	5. d	6. d	7. d	8. d	9. c	10. c
11. b	12. d	13. d	14. c	15. d	16. b	17. d	18. d	19. d	20. c
21. d	22. a	23. d	24. b	25. d	26. d	27. d	28. d	29. b	30. b
31. b	32. d	33. d	34. d	35. b	36. b	37. a	38. a	39. c	40. a
41. b	42. d	43. d	44. d	45. d	46. c	47. a	48. d	49. d	50. d
51. b	52. b	53. c	54. a	55. d	56. b	57. d	58. a	59. b	60. a
61. b	62. b	63. c							

Chapter 2

1. c	2. b	3. d	4. b	5. b	6. d	7. d	8. a	9. d	10. b
11. c	12. c	13. d	14. b	15. a	16. d	17. b	18. c	19. d	20. d
21. d	22. b	23. b	24. c	25. a	26. d	27. d	28. d	29. d	30. a
31. a	32. d								

Chapter 3

1. a	2. d	3. b	4. a	5. b	6. c	7. c	8. d	9. b	10. d
11. d	12. d	13. d	14. d	15. b	16. b	17. d	18. c	19. b	20. d
21. a	22. c	23. d	24. d	25. d	26. c	27. b	28. d	29. d	30. c
31. d	32. d								

Chapter 4

1. b	2. d	3. d	4. d	5. d	6. c	7. d	8. a	9. c	10. d
11. a	12. a	13. a							

Chapter 5

1. c	2. b	3. c	4. d	5. d	6. a	7. d	8. d	9. c	10. a
11. a	12. b	13. d	14. b	15. c	16. d	17. c	18. d	19. b	20. d
21. d									

Chapter 6

1. d	2. d	3. d	4. c	5. b	6. d	7. d	8. c	9. d	10. c
11. d	12. a	13. d	14. c	15. a	16. d	17. a	18. d	19. d	

Chapter 7

1. b	2. a	3. b	4. b	5. d	6. b	7. d	8. a	9. a	10. d
11. b									

Chapter 8

1. a	2. c	3. b	4. d	5. a	6. d	7. d	8. b	9. d	10. a
11. a	12. d	13. d	14. c	15. a	16. d	17. a	18. c	19. c	20. a
21. a	22. d	23. d	24. a	25. d	26. b	27. d	28. c	29. a	

ANSWER KEY

Chapter 9
1. c   2. a   3. d   4. b   5. d   6. c   7. a   8. b   9. b   10. a
11. d   12. d   13. d   14. d   15. d   16. c   17. d   18. d   19. c   20. d
21. a   22. b   23. b   24. a   25. d   26. d   27. d   28. a   29. d   30. d
31. d   32. d   33. a   34. b

Chapter 10
1. d   2. d   3. b   4. d   5. d   6. d   7. d   8. b   9. d   10. c
11. d   12. b   13. d   14. d

www.ingramcontent.com/pod-product-compliance
Lightning Source LLC
Chambersburg PA
CBHW082049230426
43670CB00016B/2834